Out of the Mouths
of Slaves

African American Language
and Educational Malpractice

UNIVERSITY OF TEXAS PRESS
AUSTIN

Out of
the Mouths
of Slaves

JOHN BAUGH
FOREWORD BY WILLIAM LABOV

Requests for permission to reproduce material from this work should be sent to
PERMISSIONS, UNIVERSITY OF TEXAS PRESS, P.O. BOX 7819, AUSTIN, TX 78713-7819.

(∞) The paper used in this publication meets the minimum requirements of American
National Standard for Information Sciences—Permanence of Paper for Printed Library
Materials, ANSI Z39.48-1984.

Frontispiece illustration courtesy Institute of Texan Cultures. #73-1520. Engraving
published in *Harper's Weekly,* Feb. 26, 1870, p. 141.

PERMISSION TO REPRINT HAS BEEN GIVEN BY THE FOLLOWING:
CHAPTER 1 originally appeared as "Some Common Misconceptions about Black Street
Speech" in *Touchstone* 13 (1988) 7–9. CHAPTER 2 originally appeared as "Language and Race:
Some Implications for Linguistic Science" in *Linguistics: The Cambridge Survey, Vol. No. 4,
Language: The Social Cultural Context.* Reprinted with permission from Cambridge
University Press. CHAPTER 3 originally appeared as "Why *What Works* Hasn't Worked for
Nontraditional Students" in *The Journal of Negro Education* 57:3 (1988) 417–430. Copyright
© 1988 Howard University. All rights reserved. CHAPTER 4 originally appeared as "Design
and Implementation of Language Arts Programs for Speakers of Nonstandard English" in
The Writing Needs of Linguistically Different Students, Bruce Cronnell, ed., Los Alamitos, CA,
1981, 17–43. CHAPTER 6 originally appeared as "Language Diversity and Justice in America:
Growing Complexities in a Traditional National Paradox" in *Urban Resources* 2.3 (Spring
1985) 31–34, 61. CHAPTER 7 originally appeared as "The Politics of Black Power Handshakes" in *Natural History* (Oct. 1978) 34–40. CHAPTER 8 originally appeared as "The
Politicization of Changing Terms of Self-Reference among American Slave Descendants"
in *American Speech* 66.2 (1991) 133–146. CHAPTER 9 originally appeared as "*Steady:* Progres-
sive Aspect in Black Vernacular English" in *American Speech* 59.1 (1984) 3–12. CHAPTER 10
originally appeared as "Discourse Functions for *Come* in Black English Vernacular" in *Texas
Linguistics Forum* 31 (1988) 42–49. CHAPTER 11 originally appeared as "Hypocorrection:
Mistakes in Production of Vernacular African American English as a Second Dialect" in
Language and Communication 12:3–4 (1992) 317–326, © 1992 with permission from Elsevier
Science. CHAPTER 12 originally appeared as "Perceptions within a Variable Paradigm" in
Focus on the USA, Edgar W. Schneider, ed. Amsterdam/Philadelphia: John Benjamins, 1996,
169–182.

Library of Congress Cataloging-in-Publication Data
Baugh, John, 1949–
    Out of the mouths of slaves : African American language and educational malpractice /
John Baugh.—1st ed.
        p.   cm.
    Includes bibliographical references and index.
    ISBN 0-292-70872-6 (alk. paper).—
    ISBN 0-292-70873-4 (pbk. : alk. paper)
    1. Afro-Americans—Language.   2. English language—Social aspects—United
States.   3. Afro-Americans—Education—Language arts.   4. Afro-Americans—Social
conditions.   5. Slaves—United States—Language.   6. Black English.   7. American-
isms.   I. Title.
PE3102.N42B39   1999
427′.973′08996—dc21   98-28384

In loving tribute to

Dr. Barbara Goore Baugh—Mom
and
Dr. J. G. Baugh—Dad

CONTENTS

Part 4   Linguistic Dimensions of African American Vernacular English

Part 5   Conclusion

FOREWORD
William Labov

Everyone who has grown up in the United States knows that racial relations are at the center of the social problems of our society, whatever view he or she may take about the causes of those problems. We observe a growing gap between rich and poor, a growing percentage of the population in prison, as well as the disorganization of family life and the deterioration of housing, services, and, above all, education in the inner cities. That part of the citizenry who do not place the blame for these problems on the descendants of slaves are more or less in agreement that institutional racism is the generating cause. They reject the view that social and educational failure in the inner city is the result of laziness or the intellectual inferiority of African Americans. Yet among these people of good will, many are ready to apply these same labels to the language of African Americans. The dominant view among educators is that the inadequacies of African American language are the main obstacles to educational advancement. This book is a powerful counter-statement which should change the minds of many who hold such views.

Of all those scholars who have written on the language of African Americans, John Baugh has perhaps the broadest and the most active view. The final chapter of this book begins with the firm statement, "In my view linguistic science is socially active." Throughout this volume, the reader will gain a perspective on the debates about African American language in their full social context, a perspective from which the normal academic barriers are rarely visible. As one example, Baugh's treatment of the terms that African Americans use for themselves begins by questioning whether the public statement of one man—the Reverend Jesse Jackson—could possibly have led to a linguistic shift of the entire community.

Perhaps the most powerful of all the chapters in this book is the one that deals with "educational malpractice." To many of us, this is a new and startling idea. Baugh presents a rich array of case histories and explores the concept in detail. Basically a supporter of efforts to accelerate Standard English proficiency, he raises questions as to whether those objecting to educators who advocate Ebonics could accuse them of educational malpractice. It seems likely that such legal challenges to the educational system may play a major role in the development of educational policy. As someone who shudders at the excesses of medical malpractice lawsuits, I find myself wondering why malpractice suits have never been brought against the schools in Harlem and Philadelphia, which regularly fail to teach children to read.

These discussions of social issues rest on a firm knowledge of what African American language is really like. Baugh's credentials as one of the leading investigators of that language are well established. His linguistic research in the Pacoima community of Southern California, reported in his *Black Street Speech,* added several new dimensions to our understanding of the home language of African Americans. Baugh was the first to demonstrate that African American vernacular English (AAVE) shows its clearest and most distinctive form among adults who work and live with other African Americans. He never makes the error of treating AAVE as an invariant stereotype, in which every bit of variation is a borrowing from "standard English." Throughout this volume, Baugh moves with confidence among the intricate linguistic details of AAVE grammar, distinguishing what is invariant from what is variable. This book brings together two of his most important and innovative studies of that grammar: the treatment of the auxiliary *steady,* and his empirical studies of the modal *come.*

Many of the studies of AAVE, including some of the best, are based entirely on observations of the vernacular. Baugh's goes beyond the analysis of variation, and introduces a wide variety of controlled experiments, which tell us about the community's interpretation of the linguistic features we are dealing with. In all of his grammatical analyses, Baugh explores meaning and evaluation through this experimental route. Among the most informative of these is his survey of reactions to the terms that African Americans use for themselves. In these results, we get a broad panorama of the recent history of community reactions, which gives a greater depth of understanding than we could ever gain from isolated quotations.

Though Baugh's use of scientific method is an essential component of this book, no reader will see it as having been written in the laboratory. The heart of Baugh's method is ethnographic. It is because he personally knows the people who speak this language that he can lay out a realistic political and cultural position. The most powerful and effective statements in this book are the direct quotations from those whom he has interviewed over the years. Indeed, their eloquence is a powerful challenge to anyone who would try to restate what they have to say in academic language:

> It ain't no white people really care about us, cause if they did they wouldn't try to make you turn you into a white person, they'd take you like you is.

As I have found myself, it isn't easy for the linguist to compete with the speakers of everyday language, from a logical or a rhetorical point of view. But many of Baugh's own formulations rise to that challenge, and I expect that we will see them quoted many times in the years to come.

PREFACE

The world was briefly transfixed on the linguistic consequences of American slavery after the Oakland school board passed a resolution declaring Ebonics to be the official language of the twenty-eight thousand African American students enrolled in that district. The ensuing media frenzy exposed a myriad of linguistic myths and fallacies across the political spectrum. The Afro-centric scholarship that gave rise to Ebonics eventually collapsed under the combined weight of political pressure and the untenable linguistic hypothesis that a speech community can be defined in racial terms. Conservative pundits produced some highly predictable platitudes regarding language, intelligence, and the work ethic, and a broad range of moderates were simply confused by Oakland's Ebonics aspirations. What possible reason could Oakland educators offer in support of their extreme linguistic assertions?

The Linguistic Society of America (LSA) entered the fray in January 1997, adopting a resolution that affirmed the linguistic integrity and grammatical coherence of African American vernacular English (AAVE), but these efforts were misunderstood by many in the general public who dismissed the scientific foundations of the LSA resolution as mere evidence of an academic exercise in political correctness. Several critics presented demeaning portraits of linguistic analyses pertaining to American slave descendants. Ironically, studies of AAVE are among the most advanced of any branch of sociolinguistic inquiry by virtue of the fact that several of Labov's (1972a,b) seminal linguistic contributions are derived from studies of linguistic change and variation among African Americans.

While many social scientists have either ignored or marginalized African American behaviors, the formal development of Labovian sociolinguistic theory utilized African American data as a primary source. Linguists and sociolinguists represent an extremely small portion of the population, and the combination of political and social events that have surrounded the Ebonics controversy and other racially charged public episodes demand that scholars provide clarification whenever possible.

This book strives to offer a modest contribution in that formidable quest, a quest that has captured the passion and imagination of younger to older scholars from various racial backgrounds who realize that the linguistic consequences of American slavery are unlike the linguistic heritage of those whose American ancestors were never enslaved or subjected to the inferior social circumstances of racial segregation and educational apartheid.

As such the intended audience for this book is simultaneously eclectic and narrowly focused—"eclectic" in the sense that a broad range of topics and analyses are surveyed herein; and "narrowly focused" in the sense that studies of AAVE in social, educational, and linguistic terms are represented. To a very large extent this work has been inspired by Labov's *Language in the Inner-City: Studies in the Black English Vernacular* (1972a). Like that text, the majority of chapters in this book have been updated and revised from earlier publications that were not originally intended to appear in book form, but which have renewed relevance in the wake of the profound linguistic misunderstanding that was displayed throughout the Ebonics controversy (Baugh 1997).

The text is divided into five parts wending from general introductory remarks through more technical linguistic analyses. Part I, Orientation, includes Chapter 1, "Some Common Misconceptions about African American Vernacular English," and Chapter 2, "Language and Race: Some Implications of Bias for Linguistic Science." Part II, The Relevance of African American Vernacular English to Education and Social Policies, begins with Chapter 3, "Why *What Works* Has Not Worked for Nontraditional Students," followed by Chapter 4, "Reading, Writing, and Rap: Lyric Shuffle and Other Motivational Strategies to Introduce and Reinforce Literacy." Chapters 5 and 6 move into matters of policy, covering "Educational Malpractice and the Ebonics Controversy," and "Linguistic Discrimination and American Justice." Taken together, these chapters will be of considerable interest to educators and policy makers who seek alternative solutions to the intractable patterns of educational underachievement that still plague far too many low-income and minority students.

Part III, Cross-cultural Communication in Social Context, includes Chapter 7, "The Politics of Black Power Handshakes" and Chapter 8, "Changing Terms of Self-reference among American Slave Descendants." Part IV, "Linguistic Dimensions of African American Vernacular English," reintroduces four detailed linguistic studies: Chapter 9, "*Steady:* Progressive Aspect in African American Vernacular English," provides an account of *steady* and its functional grammatical role, and Chapter 10, "*Come* Again: Discourse Functions in African American Vernacular English," expands on Spears's (1982) formulation of "camouflaged forms" that have been concealed from many traditional linguistic studies of standard English. The remaining linguistic chapters are socially relevant: Chapter 11, "Hypocorrection: Mistakes in the Production of African American Vernacular English as a Second Dialect," will probably hold most appeal for linguists, and sociolinguists in particular, because that chapter describes a highly specialized process whereby some African Americans exceed vernacular norms in their quest to produce nonstandard English as a secondary dialect. Chapter 12, "Linguistic Perceptions in Black and White: Racial Identification Based on Speech," is an experimental study; a host of African American and non–African American speakers were recorded and then given racial classifications by judges who made their decisions based exclusively on the sound of the speaker's voice. The experiment included some bidialectal informants who, much like highly trained actors, can produce standard English or AAVE at will with considerable proficiency. That evidence, in turn, is presently being used in support of new research on housing discrimination based on speech.

The book ends with a single concluding chapter in Part V that explores "Research Trends for African American Vernacular English: Anthropology, Education, and Linguistics." It seeks to alert readers to the robust scholarly traditions associated with some outstanding research on this topic. That review is not comprehensive, however, and does not fully address the tremendous contribution by scholars who study communication and human speech disorders (see Kamhi, Pollock, and Harris 1996; Seymour and

Seymour 1981). Nevertheless, Chapter 13 will direct readers toward significant studies of African American vernacular English that are described more fully within this volume.

One of the greatest joys derived from research of this kind grows from the sense of a shared mission with others who seek to provide new solutions to old, and racially sensitive, social problems. At a time when the nation seeks greater relief from racial strife and public controversies over affirmative action, this work provides linguistic diagnostics that do not rely on racial designation, but which can nevertheless be used to replace overstated and controversial racial classifications as a means to identify and assist those truly less fortunate citizens who are most in need of help.

ACKNOWLEDGMENTS

Several friends, colleagues, and organizations have made this work possible, and I owe considerable thanks to the Ford Foundation, the National Science Foundation, the National Research Council, the Consortium for Policy Research in Education, the National Center for Postsecondary Information, the Center for Advanced Studies in the Behavioral Sciences, the American Council of Learned Societies, and the University of Texas Research Institute for an eclectic combination of prior support which has made most of this research possible.

These efforts began at the University of Pennsylvania more than two decades ago, with the financial support of the Ford Foundation and the intellectual guidance of William Labov, John Fought, Dell Hymes, and Erving Goffman. Other scholars including Walt Wolfram, Ralph Fasold, John Rickford, Guy Bailey, Salikoko Mufwene, Geneva Smitherman, Faye Vaughn-Cooke, Orlando Taylor, Mary Hoover, Lisa Green, Toya Wyatt, Marcyliena Morgan, Larry Bobo, John Singler, Ana Celia Zentella, Keith Walters, Letticia Galindo, Kathleen Ferrara, Arnetha Ball, Becky Brown, Tracy Weldon, Sonja Lanehart, Michele Foster, Etta Hollins, Dennis Preston, Larry Davis, and Michael Linn have all strongly influenced my research in direct and indirect ways that do not receive adequate recognition within the text.

Susan Crawford and Susan Thomas offered wonderful editorial advice in the early stages of this project. Editors at the University of Texas Press, including Theresa May and Leslie Tingle, also offered a combination of encouragement, wisdom, and patience that has greatly enhanced this work. Thanks, too, to Sheri Englund who resolved many problems that might have otherwise prevented publication of this book. I remain particularly grateful to Nancy Richey, however, for her diligence and thoughtful commentary. Always gracious, she provided careful attention to major and minor details that ultimately sharpened my thinking—if not my prose—and had it not been for her effort I could not have completed this work.

My family remains the ultimate source of joy and inspiration in my life. Our children, Chenoa, John, and Ariél, continue to give me wonderful linguistic insights as I grow older and further from the youthful vernacular that remains the source of so much linguistic innovation; I cherish each of them and the love they continue to provide in abundance. Their gifts are resoundingly amplified by the constant love, wisdom, support, and guidance their mother, Charla, shares with understated grace. Her instinctive balance between blunt criticism and unwavering encouragement continues to enhance my thinking and the plight of nonlinguists who may not share the same excitement over phonetics or morphophonology that I routinely display in early drafts of nearly everything I write. She always thinks of you—the reader—as she repeatedly alerts me to the needs of a broader audience. At home, however, she enriches all of our lives in wondrous ways that challenge, and indeed exceed, my capacity to explain.

With heartfelt thanks to all who have been so helpful to me throughout the years, I confess that I have not always heeded the wise counsel of others, and all limitations herein are fundamentally my own.

1

PART
ONE

Orientation

Some Common Misconceptions about African American Vernacular English

Language is complex, and mastery of it is too often taken for granted. Linguists and psychologists have demonstrated that the miracle of child language acquisition is uniquely human. All normal children in every society learn to speak without the aid of formal instruction. In America we find three groups of language learners: those who learn standard English as their first language, those who learn a nonstandard dialect of English natively, and those who do not learn English as their mother tongue.

Immigrants to the United States arrive typically with little money and no knowledge of English, often preferring to speak only with others who share fluency in their mother tongue—not because they are lazy but because learning a second language can be difficult, especially if you do not have access to English language instruction. Having experienced linguistic prejudice firsthand, most of these first-generation immigrants insist that their children become "real" Americans by learning English. Such children speak to their parents in the language of their parents' native country but use English in school and with their peers. By the third generation, most immigrant families have made a complete transition to English.

It is rare to find Americans who, after three generations, have preserved their ancestral language, particularly to the exclusion of English. A European scholar told me a joke recently. He said, "What do you call a person who speaks three languages?" I said, "A trilingual." Then he said, "And what do you call a person who speaks two languages?" I said, "A bilingual." "Then what do you call a person who speaks only one language?" Not knowing the punch line, I shook my head as if to say, "No." He said, "An American."

I pointed out that the United States is not Europe, that our nation is relatively young by world standards, and that the evolution of English in the United States differs considerably from the evolution of European languages, which have survived there in support of independent nations. Although linguistic diversity existed among Indians in precolonial America, wars, disease, and other perils destroyed a large percentage of these populations and their languages.

What distinguishes linguistic evolution of English in the United States is the concentration of various dialects on the East Coast, and a so-called general American dialect in the West and Midwest. One of the primary reasons that so many different dialects of English can be found in the eastern United States is that they were settled prior to the industrial revolution by people who brought different English accents with them to this land. The industrial revolution, particularly the development of transportation, made possible the settlement of larger geographic regions where people eventually developed American dialects that covered wider territories.

Also contributing to the evolution of American English was the migration of blacks from the South after the Civil War to urban areas of the north. They took their Southern speech patterns with them, including all of the unique linguistic forms that had been incorporated into the grammatical structure of speech among slaves. Unlike most white immigrants to urban centers, who eventually adopted local dialects, blacks generally remained isolated in impoverished ghettos and as a result, retained their dialect. This physical isolation contributed to linguistic isolation and the maintenance of African American vernacular English (AAVE). The retention of unique linguistic forms, racism, and educational apartheid have since led to numerous misconceptions of this dialect, all of which amount to the opinion that all speakers of this dialect lack intelligence.

Many native speakers of standard English assume that nonstandard speakers are ignorant, lazy, and less capable intellectually. The common stereotype is that nonstandard speakers, including many blacks, could speak "properly" if only they put forth sufficient effort. This view, while perhaps understandable, is woefully uninformed and simplistic. It fails to recognize the unique status of AAVE or the linguistic consequences of slavery. While most other immigrants were able to continue to speak their ancestral language in ethnic ghettos, slaves were torn from their native communities and immediately isolated from others who shared their language. The slave traders engaged in this practice to minimize the occurrence of revolt, but the linguistic dimensions of this action continue to have consequences for many black speakers today. Historically it was illegal to teach slaves to read and write, effectively denying them access to literate standard English; this unfortunate fact has also deepened the linguistic abyss between AAVE and standard English.

Many speakers of black English view this dialect from an entirely different perspective: they value it. Their personal and cultural identities are closely linked to the language of their friends, family, and forebears. And AAVE symbolizes racial solidarity. As long as the adoption of standard English is perceived to be an abandonment of black culture, an African American vernacular will continue to survive, and it will do so despite perceptions that black speech is ignorant.

An African American woman I interviewed many years ago stated her case as follows:

> You just can never forget that slavery was a bitch from the get-go. Slaves didn't get no schoolin and they ain't never really given us [African Americans] equal opportunities, so how we supposed to talk like white folks, and why would we want to? It ain't no white people really care about us, cause if they did they wouldn't try to make you turn into a white person, they'd take you like you is. But they don't do that. All my teachers in school kept tellin me, "If you don't speak proper, you won't get a job." That's bullshit! I know some Brothers that went to college—y'know, they did the "white thing," with good grades and good English, and they still have problems on the job. They done tol me about this Brother who did all the work for a white boy at his job, and then they [the Whites] lied on his ass when the boss found out and he was fired, and nobody tried to help him. How can you trust motherfuckers that do shit like that, and then they say we stupid cause we don't talk proper. Talkin proper don't feel natural to me, but that don't make me stupid—I see what's goin on, and I see what's comin down, and it ain't got nothin to do with how we talk. It's all about money, power, and politics—plain and simple!

Several linguists also view black dialects from a different perspective; they see a coherent language system. For example, in AAVE we observe sentences like the following, with *be*:

They be standin on the corner.

He be talkin when the teacher be talkin.

From a linguistic point of view, this use of *be* performs grammatical work. In African American vernacular these sentences convey habitual activities. By contrast, the standard form *is* will be used instead of *be* to convey momentary actions. The difference between "He be happy" and "He is happy" is that the latter conveys a momentary state while the former refers to a perpetual state of happiness.

Imagine the confusion confronting a black child in school who is trying to use standard English to convey a habitual state or event. Under such circumstances it would be difficult for the child not to use his or her native grammar. *Be* provides a grammatical tool that is unavailable to speakers of standard English. In addition to all that AAVE shares with other dialects of English, it has unique grammatical forms that serve important communicative functions; it is far from being an impoverished dialect. Despite all that linguistics has been able to teach us, however, black English continues to stigmatize speakers as "uneducated" members of society.

The persistence of AAVE and the misconceptions about it pose a challenge to our society. Should some citizens be discriminated against because of our collective linguistic ignorance? Educators or employers who assume that blacks are inferior intellectually on the basis of their speech may restrict their access to educational and economic opportunities. And although we may believe that our misconceptions about AAVE are linguistic, they are fundamentally racial and lead even scientists and scholars to grossly erroneous conclusions about the intelligence of black people.

Language and Race

Some Implications of Bias for Linguistic Science

The relationship between language and racial groups has both a biological and a political dimension. The biological dimension first emerged historically as distinct genetic characteristics evolved among various human tribes in relative geographical isolation. Thus, in the typical case, language and race were originally correlated directly. But throughout history, linguistic change has been both rapid and drastic in comparison with the stability of distinctive racial groups. Thus the relative status and life expectancy of a language have come to be much more a function of the political and economic circumstances of its speakers than of their race per se. Indeed, the speech communities of influential world languages like English, Spanish, French, and Russian are *multi*racial, a fact that reflects their global expansion and great political and economic influence.

Whatever the evolutionary correlation may be between race and language, linguists hold all races—and the languages of their speakers—to be equal. Franz Boas eloquently stated the case for the equality of race and Edward Sapir for equality of language:

> I believe the present state of our knowledge justifies us in saying that, while individuals differ, biological differences between races are small. There is no reason to believe that one race is by nature so much more intelligent, endowed with great will power, or emotionally more stable than another that the difference would materially influence its culture. (Boas 1940, 13–14)

> When it comes to linguistic form, Plato walks with the Macedonian swineherd, Confucius with the head-hunting savage of Assam. (Sapir 1921, 219)

This linguistic ideal of equality among languages and the various races has never been reflected in social terms. Domination of some groups over others has been the rule rather than the exception throughout history. We know all too well that some languages or dialects have come to be associated with the social status of the people who employ them. Bloomfield's observations regarding different groups within a speech community are as relevant now as they were over a half-century ago:

> We shall examine first the simpler case, as it appears in the United States. The most striking line of cleavage in our speech is one of social class. Children who are born into the homes of privilege, in the way of wealth, tradition, or education, become native speakers of what is known as "good" English; the linguist prefers to give it the noncommittal name of standard English. Less fortunate children become native speakers of "bad" or "vulgar" or, as the linguist prefers to call it, nonstandard English. (Bloomfield 1933, 48)

The social division of dialects, particularly along racial lines, is obviously not unique to the United States. Other examples abound from around the globe—legacies of the incontrovertible political and economic dimensions of postcolonial racism, among other pertinent factors. Racism has a linguistic aspect, of course; racists believe that their language (and most other aspects of their culture) is superior to those of the "inferior" races. Such an attitude, if supported by political domination, whether overt or covert, is used to justify attempts to impose various doctrines on racially subordinate groups. Ironically, these policies are usually offered in the name of "improving" the plight of less fortunate peoples.

JENSEN'S HYPOTHESIS AND THE
LINGUISTIC SOCIETY OF AMERICA RESPONSE

Linguistic science is uniquely equipped to redress the language dimensions of morally indefensible racist ideologies wherever they are found. While linguists, of course, have no special expertise on the political factors that support racism, they are in a unique position to expose racially loaded fallacies about language and mind. The most notorious is Arthur Jensen's (1969) claim that black children are intellectually inferior to white children on *genetic* grounds. Since Jensen's notions were based in part on fallacies about black language, linguists were ideally suited to combat them. And they did just that. The Linguistic Society of America (LSA) in 1972 endorsed a widely publicized resolution by Anthony Kroch and William Labov that exposed the flimsy intellectual basis of Jensen's ideas. Given its importance and the fact that it can serve as a model for future struggles against overtly racist ideas, it is worth citing in full:

> The writings of Arthur Jensen which argue that many lower class people are born with an inferior type of intelligence contain unfounded claims which are harmful to many members of our society. Jensen and others have introduced into the arena of public debate the theory that the population of the United States is divided by genetic inheritance into two levels of intellectual ability: one defined by the ability to form concepts freely, the other limited in this area and confined primarily to the association of ideas.
>
> Because this theory, if accepted, would necessarily alter educational policy and seriously affect the lives of many of our fellow citizens, and because linguists are familiar with a large body of evidence which bears on the question, the Linguistic Society of America issues the following statement and resolution, representing the considered professional opinion of scientific linguists. The following conclusions are based on facts generally known to linguists:
>
> 1. By an early age, children learn without direct instruction, on the basis of the speech that they hear, the largest part of the grammar of their native language. This grammar is the knowledge of a hierarchically structured set of relations, used by the speaker to produce and understand an unlimited number of simple and complex sentences.
> 2. No one language or dialect, standard or nonstandard, is known to be

significantly more complex than another in its basic grammatical appa-
ratus. Linguists have not yet discovered any speech community with
a native language that can be described as conceptually or logically
primitive, inadequate or deficient.

3. The nonstandard dialects of English spoken by lower class families
   in the inner cities of the United States are fully formed languages with
   all of the grammatical structure necessary for logical thought. Statements to the contrary by some educational psychologists are misinter-
   pretations of superficial differences in the means of expression between these dialects and standard English.

4. No theory yet developed by linguists or psychologists can account sat-
   isfactorily for children's language learning ability. It is generally agreed
   that the mere association of ideas is not sufficient. The minimal ability
   necessary to learn and to speak any human language includes native
   skills of much higher order of magnitude than those used in the laboratory tests offered in evidence for Dr. Jensen's view.

On the basis of these generally recognized conclusions of linguistic investigation, linguists agree that all children who have learned to speak a human language have a capacity for concept formation beyond our present
power to analyze; that language learning abilities indicate that the nature
and range of human intelligence is not yet understood or well-measured by
any current testing procedure; that tests which may have some value in
predicting later performance in school should not be interpreted as measures of intelligence in any theoretically coherent sense of the word; that
to attribute a limited level of "associational intelligence" to a sizable section of our population is a serious misconception of the nature of human
intelligence. (Kroch & Labov 1972, 17–18)

FARRELL'S REINTERPRETATION
OF JENSEN'S HYPOTHESIS

Misconceptions about language, race, and intelligence are not in general as
blatant as Jensen's. But even where such misconceptions lend inadvertent
credence to racist myths and ideologies, linguists can—and I believe
should—devote the necessary time to dispelling these errors.

To illustrate this point, we will consider a case from the United States,
where some well-intentioned scholars have advocated ill-conceived language policies in an effort to help black children improve their IQ scores.

Thomas J. Farrell (1984a) advocates that we revive the old McGuffey readers to help black Americans attain higher degrees of literacy, and proposes as well a series of audiovisual exercises and platitudes about how blacks need to apply themselves to study in order to learn. But Farrell's suggestion ignores the differences between standard and nonstandard English as contributing to the black students' lower test scores. Farrell, like so many others, appears to be laboring under the misconception that language differences are irrelevant in the testing situation, and thus implicitly supports the idea that blacks are intrinsically "less intelligent" than whites.[1]

The most insidious aspect of Farrell's work, particularly his 1983 paper "IQ and Standard English," is his resuscitation of many of the misconceptions found in Jensen's original hypothesis. Farrell, to be sure, does not posit genetic deficiencies. In their place, he finds "literacy deficiencies." For example, he finds that literacy and the attainment of certain grammatical structures found in standard English are required for abstract thought.[2] Only then does the cognitive transformation take place that allows speakers to move from an "oral mentality" to a "literate mentality."

THE LINGUISTS' RESPONSE TO FARRELL

Many of the assumptions that Farrell draws upon to support this hypothesis are incompatible with established principles of linguistic science. Consider, for example, the following passage from his 1983 paper:

> The development of abstract thinking depends on learning (1) the full standard deployment of the verb "to be" and (2) embedded modification and (3) subordination. Historically these are the three features of language that developed as the ancient Greeks moved from oral to literate composing, which resulted in the development of abstract thinking. IQ test scores reveal that black ghetto children have not developed the power of abstract thinking, and they do not speak standard English. (1983, 481)

He sees rational thought essentially as a gift of the Greek alphabet: "Abstract thinking did not develop with the all-consonant alphabet; it developed only with the Greek alphabet . . . the development of letters for vowel sounds was important for the development of abstract thinking" (1984a, 475). How does Farrell measure abstract thinking? His debt to Jensen is explicit: "IQ tests used by Jensen and other educational psychologists [are a] 'valid' and 'reliable' measure of abstract thinking" (1983, 471).

Confusion about language permeates Farrell's work. For example, he expresses some skepticism about currently prevailing views in linguistic theory:

> I know that one theory of linguistics postulates that meaning is conveyed through so-called deep structures, not surface forms. But I for one do not believe this is true because I have known too many people who are very poor readers and who also do not know standard English. Conversely, I have not encountered any good readers who do not know standard English. (1984b, 822)

Such opinions confuse very different cognitive processes and do not take functional (ethno)linguistic considerations into account. For example, speech and writing involve radically different neurological processes, each of which is dependent to varying degrees on a set of unpredictable communicative events. It would seem, then, that Farrell compounds Jensen's errors by adding a set of misconceptions about language and cognition.

The assumption that literacy deficiencies are at the heart of the issue is tenuous at best. Contrary to Farrell, substantial evidence exists that abstract thought was available to humans long before the representation of vocalic phonemes in the Greek alphabet. For example, primitive tool and meta-tool[3] making represent incontrovertible evidence of abstract thought among early humans. No one can deny the importance of writing in various cultures around the world. Yet literacy is distributed according to capricious political and economic variables that are subject to constant changes, while the cognitive interplay of *langue* and *parole,* so central to abstract thought, is available to all normal children in language acquisition. In fact, it is the miracle of language acquisition itself that distinguishes our species most strongly from all others. While all normal children learn to talk, only some are provided with adequate opportunities to master literacy. Opportunity, or lack thereof, is the critical factor. In cognitive terms, literacy is more comparable to other skilled behaviors, like artistic talent, that develop and improve with the right combination of time, training, and economic support. Without the proper opportunity, children will not become literate because literacy is not inherent or innate. This contrasts sharply with oral language development among normal children, which is universal regardless of race, creed, or national origin.

2

PART TWO

The Relevance of African American Vernacular English to Education and Social Policies

Why *What Works* Has Not Worked for Nontraditional Students

The principal contribution that the federal government can make [to public education] is to supply good information to the American people. . . . Armed with good information, the American people can be trusted to fix their own schools.

—William Bennett

If we ever hope to overcome linguistic ignorance and uninformed assumptions about race and language (see Chapter 2), then educators must participate in systemic reforms that will ensure educational equity. Toward this end it is necessary to update outmoded thinking on these matters. At first blush the preceding quotation makes considerable sense, but in the face of long-standing bias against students of color, we need more comprehensive ways to help less fortunate students.

In 1985, former Secretary of Education William J. Bennett directed his staff to assemble a condensed booklet on public education entitled *What Works: Research about Teaching and Learning*. He characterized the publication as "a distillation of a large body of scholarly research in the field of education" (p. v); however, those of us who have devoted our lives and research to the goals of educational parity will find very little in it in the way of useful information for minority students. One would expect a director of national educational policies to recognize that our citizens represent a culturally pluralistic society; *What Works* fails to acknowledge this reality.

What Works begins with a detailed introduction by Chester E. Finn, Jr., former assistant secretary of research and improvement, who was assigned the task of producing the document. Anticipating the type of criticism I offer here, his introduction includes no claim that the study made an effort to be comprehensive, and he admits that many of its findings appear obvious. Of greatest concern to me, however, is the claim that *What Works* has "tried to deal with the 'general' or 'usual' or 'average' situation . . ." (p. 3). But to strive for homogenized educational policies in a diverse and continually changing society is both futile and misleading. On a more positive note, Finn directs readers to such other resources as libraries and the Education Research Information Clearinghouse (ERIC) system as means by which they may gain broader perspectives.

Nevertheless, he posits a rhetorical question that affirms his quest for renewed federalism: "Why does the report contain so few specific recommendations about actions that should be taken?" (p. 3). Finn observes that specific practices and policies are the responsibility of parents, schools, and the states; "it is not the place of the federal government to interfere" (p. 4). Interference, though, should not be confused with the essential role the federal government could play in helping parents, schools, and states perform in responsible ways.

Despite the position taken by *What Works* on the role of government in education, we must look to history to reaffirm the vital contribution that the federal government makes to ensure that states, for example, offer adequate education to their citizens regardless of race, creed, gender, handicap, or national origin. *What Works* proceeds on the assumption that educational policies are somehow equal from one state to another, as well as among school districts within states, when the facts of declining educational outcomes present stark evidence to the contrary. Some states and school districts offer outstanding public education, while others—for any number of social, historical, and economic reasons—do not. In light of this educational disparity, the federal government can, and I believe should, do more to promote specific standards of academic achievement nationally. Such an effort would ensure that all citizens have access to schools that meet minimum, high national standards.

During my early fieldwork in poor black neighborhoods in Los Angeles, I would ask parents about the quality of education their children received. I would also raise hypothetical questions regarding prospects for change and improvement in local schools. All parents I interviewed wanted their children to receive a quality education, and very often "quality" meant educational services that are rare or nonexistent in inner-city schools. Parents expressed their desire for small class enrollments, funds for school outings, the most experienced and dedicated teachers, a full library, and greater teacher outreach to parents, among other things. These parents were armed with the knowledge of "what works," but they felt powerless to influence the local and state bureaucracies that controlled the educational destiny of their children. These parents were also aware of their educational limitations and expressed considerable frustration when their own illiteracy prevented them from being more directly involved in the education of their children. A mother of six described the situation to me as follows:

> J: If you could change the educational system, you know, if you were in charge, what would you do?
> M: I don't like that I can't help my kids myself. I need the teachers to help me learn how to help my kids, but you can't always count on help from the schools. I ain't sayin all the teachers be bad, but it's enough of 'em bad that you can't count on them lookin out for your child. So I would have all the teachers work with the parents.

Many African American students do not feel, or have not felt, that schools are truly beneficial to their lives, and many African American parents have personal memories of racist encounters in schools. The lingering legacy of educational apartheid has weakened essential bonds between numerous parents, teachers, and school administrators, yet Finn correctly observes that students are most likely to succeed when cooperation among these three parties is strong.

In three sections—Home, Classroom, School—*What Works* purports to offer citizens and parents a guide to educational success. Many of the suggestions in *What Works* are valuable, but as I will demonstrate in the remainder of this chapter, their impact on the educational lives of less fortunate students will be minimal or nil until the realities of poverty, racism, and unequal economic investments in education are recognized.

The very first research finding presented in the "Home" section of *What Works* states, "Parents are their children's first and most influential teachers. What parents do to help their children learn is more important to academic success than how well off the family is" (p. 7).

The implied dismissal of economic status is somewhat valid, but it is also misleading. In research that I conducted previously to evaluate successful minorities, each informant indicated that someone took an early interest in his or her education. Parents were not always the ones responsible for this academic oversight; grandparents, siblings, other relatives, church leaders, and family friends often performed this function. This was especially the case in families in which caring parents had themselves been denied access to adequate education. Such parents sought outside assistance, although they were not directly involved in the day-to-day monitoring of their children's academic progress. They were attempting to ensure greater success for their children, much like wealthy parents who send their children to the finest private schools. Parental neglect will hurt the education of any child, regardless of background, but it should also be clear that those who are "better off" have a greater opportunity to improve their children's chances for academic success. Poorer families must make a tremendous sacrifice in order to provide sufficient assistance to their children to ensure comparable success.

The second research finding for "Home" states: "The best way for parents to help their children become better readers is to read to them—even when they are very young. Children benefit most from reading aloud when they discuss stories, learn to identify letters and words, and talk about the meanings of words" (p. 9).

Public awareness of declining literacy has been heightened by many books, articles, and television advertising and programs. The Advertising Council in affiliation with the Coalition for Literacy, and many other national organizations, has increased public awareness of this problem; indeed, the publication *Becoming a Nation of Readers* (Binkley et al. 1986) was largely responsible for raising public awareness of declining national literacy. Readers of this text are probably all too familiar with the problem: if parents are not readers, they cannot read to their children (Kozol 1991).

Adults in America tend to hide reading difficulties if they have them. They are embarrassed by the fact that they have not mastered basic literacy skills, and many are adept at keeping this fact concealed from employers, employees, and their relatives; others are not capable of maintaining such a facade. This problem is deeply personal to me because I recently discovered that some of my oldest and dearest relations had difficulty reading. They had managed to keep this hidden from me for most of my life. It was my personal experience that loving adults would pretend to read stories to me as a child, which is why I thought they could read. These older relatives would present a flowing story to me as if they were actually fluent readers. Since I was too young to know the difference, I simply assumed that they could read, which was the objective of their loving hoax. The essential point is simple though, and worth repeating. If parents cannot read, they will not be able to teach their children to read, or to monitor the development of their children's literacy.

FIGURE 1.   A model of socially stratified dialects of a language.

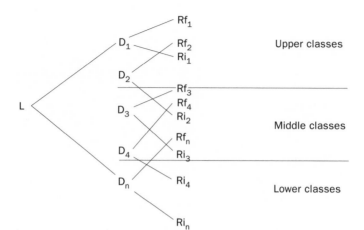

Illiteracy is socially stratified; so too are the dialects that compose most of the world's languages. The models illustrated in Figures 1 and 2 include temporal dimensions that were omitted from my previous studies of black street speech (Baugh 1983). Other linguists, and discourse analysts in particular (Tannen 1982; Chafe 1980; Ong 1982), have studied differences between verbal and written discourse. By placing human discourse in its ecological context (Haugen 1972), we are well situated to add the other dimensions that can distinguish between formal written discourse, produced on one occasion, from informal speech by the same person produced on another occasion.

Figure 1 illustrates the case where L represents a language that consists of several socially stratified dialects $(D_1–D_n)$, where D_1 corresponds to the highest social class[es] of speakers, and D_n represents the lowest socioeconomic groups of L speakers. Speakers of any given dialect (D_x) will also exhibit a range of formal to informal speech, where Rf_x represents the formal register of speech (for D_x) and Ri_x represents the informal register for the same dialect. In addition to this range of formality, Figure 1 also illustrates the differences in professional and personal discourse within any specified communicative event (Hymes 1964). Figure 2 provides a taxonomy for a fluctuating range of formal to informal discourse, which may be written or spoken, for personal or professional reasons; any communicative event can be located within the cube, and any given communicative event can navigate within the cube during its course.

These illustrations are offered in support of an obvious fact: parents

FIGURE 2.   A taxonomy of different discourse functions.

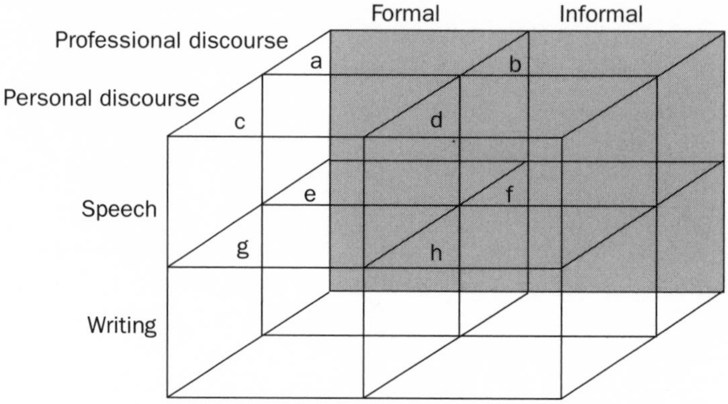

who are not only wealthy but also members of dominant linguistic groups can offer clear educational, linguistic, and perhaps occupational advantages to their children in ways that speakers of nondominant dialects of the same language cannot. The models illustrated in Figures 1 and 2 fail to capture the complexity of linguistic diversity in the United States, however, because only one language is considered at a time. Those students for whom English is not a native language face barriers that differ considerably from those faced by speakers of nonstandard English (Galindo 1995; Valdés 1996; Zentella 1981).

The last research finding in "Home" is closely linked to adult literacy: "Children improve their reading ability by reading a lot. Reading achievement is directly related to the amount of reading children do in and out of school" (p. 11).

Children are far more likely to read a lot if their parents are also readers. When parental literacy skills are weak or nonexistent, then those of the children are likely to suffer. Some poor parents have developed unique strategies to cope with this dilemma; they locate tutors for their children, and they reinforce the suggestions offered by those tutors. One of my early informants discussed her strategy to support her children's education.

> D: Now, I'm gon tell you the truth. I didn't go past the fourth grade back to Louisiana, and I was lucky to get that cause my mama had nine kids and as soon as we could work, y'know, to help the family, we was out makin money. Well, I don't want that for my kids, and up to Oakland—that's where my kids and me live—we kept an eye on the schools.

J: How'd you do that?

D: We got us a whole group of Mamas that worked with the school, and we got us a lawyer to help us deal with them, and she knew how to deal with readin. So we kept our kids in school, and this lawyer helped us to help our kids, and deal with the teachers and the school board.

This mother clearly wants her children to receive a good education even though she does not have the personal literacy skills to lend direct assistance. By banding together with other parents who shared similar concerns and then hiring an attorney to represent them and their children as an educational advocate, these African American parents adopted very creative strategies to enhance educational prospects for their children. Whenever their students would bring home memoranda from school, parents would contact their attorney, who would then read the documents and offer her best advice on how the parents should proceed. This situation is atypical; few inner-city parents can spare the resources to coordinate group hiring of attorneys as student advocates. Nevertheless, many minority parents have gone to extraordinary lengths to secure educational support for their children even though they themselves have not yet mastered literacy.

Despite the historical legacy of separate and unequal education for black Americans, many parents espouse the ideas that are advocated for the home in *What Works*: "Belief in the value of hard work, the importance of personal responsibility, and the importance of education itself contributes to greater success in school" (p. 7).

When parents have been unable to obtain a good education for themselves, they are often skeptical of the prospect that their children will benefit from equal educational opportunities. It is harder to believe in the work ethic if you believe you are devalued, and African Americans have told me on countless occasions that their contacts with teachers and the police are among their most memorable racist experiences. Whereas it is possible for a white student to attend public schools and have very little contact with minority teachers, it is nearly impossible for students of color to attend schools where significant numbers of their teachers are not white. Throughout much of my own education, for example, many racist instructors, in classes filled predominantly with white students, were openly hostile to the prospect of academic advancement by minorities. They conveyed this message overtly and covertly in direct opposition to the positive values my parents instilled in me at home.

I was more fortunate than many of my peers, because both of my parents have doctoral degrees and had the experience to confront bigoted teachers on my behalf. It is not sufficient for parents to advocate the importance of education if that message is not positively reinforced in the schools. When teachers have low expectations, based on stereotypes and prejudice, the positive efforts by parents will only lead to frustration on the part of their children.

A cooperative effort by students, their parents, and teachers is needed to truly reinforce the value of hard work and the importance of personal responsibility. If any member of this partnership is weakened, these values could become disjointed or, worse, perceived as a cruel farce.

Findings in *What Works* pertaining to "Classroom" bridge the gap between the home and the school, as the following statement indicates: "Parental involvement helps children learn more effectively. Teachers who are successful at involving parents in their children's school work are successful because they work at it" (p. 19).

The cooperation of parents and teachers is essential to successful education. My own research supports this finding; those teachers who make the effort to contact parents—on their own initiative—tend to be far more successful with their students than those who do not. This type of extraordinary professional devotion can be taxing on teachers, however, because it is often time-consuming, unrewarded, and unappreciated.

One of the elementary school teachers I interviewed in Los Angeles captured the feeling of many of her colleagues when she observed, "I make less money than the janitor and a lot less than trash collectors. I do the best job that I can in the classroom, but nobody pays for overtime, so where is the incentive to do more than I absolutely have to?" I suspect that if greater economic inducements could be offered to teachers for meeting with parents, this would be a more common practice. If teachers are not rewarded for extra effort, then it is difficult to appeal to their sense of professionalism. Many teachers resent added demands on their time without additional compensation, especially since so many other occupations offer economic incentives to employees who devote more time, attention, and energy to their jobs.

Even when teachers are committed to working with parents, some parents do not appreciate their efforts, object to the intrusion, and rebuff well-intended outreach by the teacher. In the absence of a formal policy to contact parents, agreed to by parents, teachers, and administrators, there will be an inevitable inconsistency among faculty within a school regarding the value, utility, and wisdom of such efforts.

The next finding in "Classroom" returns to literacy skills and reveals some hidden linguistic issues: "Children get a better start in reading if they are taught phonics. Learning phonics helps them to understand the relationship between letters and sounds and to 'break the code' that links words they hear with the words they see in print" (p. 21).

This finding is somewhat more complicated than it appears, especially in relation to the linguistic backgrounds of students who attend public schools. Those who learn standard English as their native dialect, those who learn a nonstandard dialect of English natively, and those whose native language is not English have different experiences in learning the phonics of English because each begins with a different phonological inventory. When I attended public school in Philadelphia and Los Angeles, for example, it was common for teachers to stress pronunciation differences between "pin" and "pen" or "tin" and ten," because many of us tended to pronounce these words the same. From a linguistic point of view the vocalic phonemes in these words were merged in my nonstandard black dialect, thereby complicating the phonics lesson. Many Hispanic students tend to add an initial /e-/ vowel before English words that begin with /s-/, which is transferred from Spanish. It is therefore common to encounter pronunciations or spellings such as "eschool" or "especial" in their English usage; again, the phonics issue is complicated.

Very few teachers have had the opportunity to study these problems from a linguistic perspective, and yet without this information the task of teaching basic literacy skills is biased in favor of students who already speak standard English.

Linguists can help teachers become more aware of linguistic differences among their students, and in so doing begin to expose some of the internal linguistic factors that cause interference between the dominant language at school and other dominant language(s) or dialect(s) that students use or encounter in their daily lives beyond the school (Labov 1994).

When academic discourse differs greatly from the language in the home, then linguistics can contribute to a rational identification of relevant linguistic differences. In the case of standard English in contrast to other nonstandard dialects (not just African American vernacular English), some differences will be relatively minor—such as intonation—while other grammatical or dialectal differences could ultimately inhibit communication.

This more complicated linguistic picture is directly related to the suggestion that "Children get more out of a reading assignment when the teacher precedes the lesson with background information and follows it with discussion" (p. 22). All too often teachers have not been given adequate training in how to work with students from heterogeneous linguistic backgrounds.

In our work with teacher education we have found it necessary to introduce basic linguistic concepts to all of the student teachers, regardless of subject area, because we have been able to identify some linguistic barriers to academic success for students from various language and dialect backgrounds. Similarly, policy makers have come to recognize that school reforms, especially in demographically complex states like California, Florida, Hawaii, New York, and Texas, among others, must take language issues into account because so many students in these states are not native speakers of English.

Two additional findings cited in *What Works* pertain directly to literacy skills and the classroom, and they are related to essential distinctions between oral and literate behavior. The first is, "Telling young children stories can motivate them to read. Storytelling also introduces them to cultural values and literary traditions before they can read, write, and talk about stories by themselves" (p. 25). The second is, "The most effective way to teach writing is to teach it as a process of brainstorming, composing, revising, and editing" (p. 27).

I tend to agree with these observations, although I too am uncertain as to how one motivates students to engage in these processes. As mentioned previously, I believe the stories that I was told as a child helped me come to enjoy books and writing even though I had no idea that my storytellers were continuing in the oral storytelling tradition. They were modeling reading behavior, and I was the happy beneficiary of this effort. One need not be a good reader in order to be a good storyteller, and direct engagement of children with adults through a good story can instill in children an essential appreciation for language, which can serve children well in schools and, eventually, in the world of work.

Brainstorming usually implies a group process, and it is during the early stages of idea formation that teachers and students need to share enough mutual sensitivity and respect to engage in productive discourse that leads toward composing. Composing, in turn, can be an individual or group activity; both steps are essential to good writing and the organization of any text. Many of the most successful teachers of writing, regardless of student background, devote considerable time and energy to these initial steps, thereby allowing students to develop (and discard) a host of ideas and giving them adequate time to compose a thesis and organize a text that supports that thesis. While many think of writing as the drafting, revising, and editing processes, genuine writing relies on curiosity and thought, depends on the effective arrangement of ideas, and often finds its success in the response of an intended audience.

I therefore agree with *What Works* regarding its emphasis on content over excessive scrutiny of questionable writing mechanics. Instruction in good writing should stress matters of thinking, clarification, and coherence first, allowing students to develop their writing. Once the content is established, then teachers or others helping with editing can draw the author's attention to "polishing" a final draft. When I was a student, far too many teachers reversed this process, focusing initially—if not exclusively—on spelling and grammar. It was rare to find writing instructors who stressed content over form.

What Works misses an essential transition that some linguists have explored for years; namely, the acquisition of literacy. More specifically, they recognize that all normal children learn to speak without the aid of formal instruction, but that very few children learn to write without direct assistance. All students need support along these lines, but many African American students need additional help because black street vernacular and academic discourse exhibit greater linguistic discrepancies than exist between spoken standard English and standard academic writing.

I have oversimplified the complexity of the transition from speech to writing, but the essential point remains: we must recognize that different students have access to different resources—economic, educational, and linguistic. These different resources are also correlated with the likelihood of student success. Educational and linguistic research can provide policy makers, educational administrators, and teachers with the information they need to help less fortunate students "catch up" to their more fortunate peers as we strive to attain educational parity for all students.

A finding pertaining to "study skills" is relevant because less fortunate students often have fewer opportunities to develop competitive study skills. *What Works* says, "The ways in which children study influence strongly how much they learn. Teachers can often help children develop better study skills" (p. 29).

Just as different students will be able to draw upon different resources for education, so too will various students encounter diverse factors that influence the circumstances under which they are allowed to study. Some children are fortunate; they have parents who have the desire, dedication, and funds to provide excellent study facilities. Other parents, who may have the same loving aspirations for their children, are not able to offer the time, funds, or energy that are needed to ensure that their children can devote sufficient time to their studies.

In the previously discussed study of successful minorities, I discovered that these individuals were allowed to devote attention to education as a primary task. When compared to peers of equal economic impoverishment, those who were successful had been provided with more time to study, while many of their friends were obliged to work or to care for other children at home.

The last finding pertaining to the classroom, regarding "assessment," reinforces the cooperative network between parents, teachers, and administrators that I stressed earlier: "Frequent and systematic monitoring of students' progress helps students, parents, teachers, administrators, and policy makers identify strengths and weaknesses in learning and instruction" (p. 43).

If all parties are involved in student assessment, there is a greater likelihood of success. Responsibilities are shared and the burden of success does not fall on individual members of the academic partnership (B. Baugh 1994). Testing is another part of assessment, but testing may also have punitive consequences for students who do not have access to adequate support. Readers of this volume may already be familiar with "performance assessment" and other educational debates regarding "opportunity to learn standards" (Darling-Hammond 1994). Educational researchers continue to explore new ways for students to demonstrate what they know and what they can do.

As schools attempt to produce students who will be suited to these information-based economies of the future, new forms of assessment will need to do more than serve their present gatekeeping function. Tests themselves continue to be biased in favor of privileged students. The results of standardized tests also show striking parallels to the social stratification of language and wealth across the United States. Educational resources are not distributed equitably, and standardized tests reflect this reality far more than they convey any meaningful evidence about differences in cognitive abilities (Carnoy 1994).

The last findings in *What Works* are devoted to "School," and it is here that differences between public and private institutions are most apparent. The text states: "The most important characteristics of effective schools are strong instructional leadership, a safe and orderly climate, schoolwide emphasis on basic skills, high teacher expectations for student achievement, and continuous assessment of pupil progress" (p. 45).

Schools are subject to a variety of factors and forces that are often beyond the control of principals, other school administrators, or teachers. The size of enrollment is just one such example. Many neighborhood schools are overcrowded, and there are few ways to eliminate this problem despite the best intentions of all interested parties. Many of my early classes were cramped, and while it would be nice to have fewer students per classroom, it is also clear that reduced funding for education has had a direct detrimental effect on this goal. The first year my home state of California spent more on prisons than on higher education was 1995.

If the culture outside of school is one where peer pressures lead to violent behavior, we should not be surprised when evidence of these cultural traits crop up in urban classrooms. In classes I attended as a young man, several students carried weapons, which detracted greatly from any sense of safety. Discipline problems were common, and many teachers were forced to invest considerable attention to class disruptions, which decreased the time devoted to education.

In addition to crowded and unsafe classrooms, the absence of discipline also contributes to low educational achievement, a relationship that *What Works* makes explicit in three related findings:

1. Schools that encourage academic achievement focus on the importance of scholastic success and on maintaining order and discipline (p. 46).
2. Schools contribute to their students' academic achievement by establishing, communicating, and enforcing fair and consistent discipline policies (p. 47).
3. Unexcused absences decrease when parents are promptly informed that their children are not attending school (p. 49).

Each of the preceding findings demonstrates the clear correlation between successful schools and student discipline, be it personal discipline regarding attendance or clear disciplinary policies to ensure safe learning environments. Having attended several public schools where discipline problems were common, I am keenly aware of the cultural pressures that reinforce disruptive behavior in the classroom, and mere calls to improve the situation are inadequate for teachers who face these problems day after day.

A simple anecdote illustrates the dimensions of the problem so many urban teachers face. When I was in graduate school one of my roommates was a high school drafting teacher at a "tough" public school. He was assigned the task of bathroom inspection, and on the day in question he discovered one of his students shooting heroin. As a responsible instructor he reported the student to the principal, who in turn expelled the student immediately from school. That evening when my roommate left the school, every window and light in his car had been smashed; he also began receiving anonymous threatening phone calls, and gun shots were fired at our house on a few nights for a couple of weeks after that.

Far too many teachers face comparable dangers in schools, and the federal government is in the best position of all to ensure that adequate funds are provided to furnish a safe environment for everyone at every school. In the absence of adequate resources there is only so much that the best principals and teachers can do. When schools are dangerous, morale is low for anyone who senses the danger. Those who are familiar with urban education will recognize that I have not exaggerated this problem, and direct attention is needed to correct the situation if we hope to salvage our schools.

Teachers who work in inner-city schools face problems that are quite different from those faced by teachers in suburban schools (Conant 1961). For example, a sharp line can be drawn between schools that require metal detectors and those that do not. Who among us would willingly send our children to a school where their physical well-being was under constant threat? Yet many parents, teachers, students, and school staff are forced to accept this reality. It is partially for this reason that I question Finn's assumptions about suggestions for teachers.

What Works states that "Teachers welcome professional suggestions about improving their work, but they rarely receive them" (p. 52). Since teachers have direct classroom contact with students, it would seem that we should value their suggestions at least as much as they might value feedback about their teaching. It is equally important to recognize the relative strengths and weaknesses of individual teachers and to capitalize on these strengths in support of their preferred teaching styles. Leadership by school principals, involved parents, and other interested parties is essential to the overall quality of life within the community of any school (McLaughlin et al. 1994).

From a linguistic point of view every school can be viewed in terms of the following categories of schoolwide or classroom linguistic demographics:

1. Native speakers of standard English = X% of students
2. Native speakers of nonstandard English = Y% of students
3. Students for whom English is not native = Z% of students

Every classroom in every school across the United States is composed of some ratio of students from the above categories; this fact is incontrovertible. Yet many of the nation's schools that are cited as being "the best" rarely have significant percentages of students who are not native speakers of standard English. Thus if a school population or the population within a given classroom is such that $X > (Y + Z)$, then academic success may be considered to be highly probable for the majority of students who attend that school. By contrast, if $Z > (X + Y)$ or $(Z + Y) > X$, then students may have greater academic difficulty. I should be quick to point out once again that these linguistic categories are socially stratified, as are the resources that are available to students who attend various schools.

This brings me to the last finding in *What Works;* it pertains to foreign language education: "The best way to learn a foreign language in school is to start early and to study it intensively over many years" (p. 57). Finn's exclusive focus on English-speaking students is unfortunate, because he presents a distorted linguistic picture at the same time he fails to recognize that "Z" students already know a "foreign language" (i.e., they did not learn English natively).

Hakuta et al. (1994), among others, have called for substantial educational reform of bilingual education to reinforce the preservation of languages other than English. Many schools have adapted two-way bilingual education programs where English-speaking students attend classes with students who do not know English; students help one another learn the other language and, under the best circumstances, they do so with considerable respect for their classmates. Reduced budgets do not bode well for students for whom English is not native (ENN), nor will their teachers fare well in a political climate that devalues languages other than English. Funds that have previously been allocated to the teaching of English are unlikely to be expanded to support the maintenance of language other than English, although in the context of the global economy it would be foolish to squander the vast international linguistic resources that so many naturalized Americans possess.

Our own work in the area of reform of language policies seeks to be comprehensive and to include speakers of nonstandard English who are currently ineligible for any federal funding to help with the (voluntary?) mastery of standard English as a second dialect. In Chapter 6 we consider some of the legal precedents that focus on these problems, but for the moment, let us return to Finn's desire to address the education of "typical" or "usual" students. Are students in categories Y and Z typical? By definition they are not. *What Works* suggests that more dissemination of research findings will allow local educators to make informed decisions that will benefit their students, yet through decades of school reform we have yet to see significant numbers of minority students achieve academic success.

Yes, more minorities than ever hold positions of social influence and stature, but America is not yet free of racial bias, gender bias, or linguistic bias. The "unusual" students who are the victims of bias in schools must find innovative ways to gain access to competitive academic skills. As Tyack and Cuban (1995) observe, efforts to reform education—like those embodied in *What Works*—are unlikely to work for less fortunate students who feel their cultural contributions go unrecognized in schools and the dominant society. How then do we motivate students who are thus defined as atypical?

Reading, Writing, and Rap

Lyric Shuffle and Other Motivational Strategies to Introduce and Reinforce Literacy

It's all too easy to criticize others who fail to fully account for the educational plight of poor African American students. It is another matter altogether to devise positive strategies to bridge the gap between oral nonstandard illiteracy and written standard literacy. There are so many schools of thought on these issues that I dare not delve into the pervasive literacy debates that saturate the educational literature. The "back to basics" movement, which strikes me as far more ideological than substantive, has had a growing political impact across the country as advocates and detractors align themselves behind the academic philosophies they find most appealing.

My ideas in this area do not grow—in any exclusive sense—from traditional research within the academy; rather, they were spawned during years of fieldwork in minority communities across the country. Far from the common negative stereotypes of welfare parents who are portrayed through mass media, I observed numerous grassroots efforts to help poor minority students who attended inner-city schools. Some of these ventures were bolstered by community-based organizations (see McLaughlin et al. 1994), while others were initiated by concerned local parents, and still others came from within schools or school districts. As described in the previous chapter, I have interviewed parents who adopted communal strategies to combat illiteracy, marshalling their limited resources to bolster educational prospects for their children.

Lyric Shuffle games were first designed with those parents in mind, and the recognition that although their children wanted to become educated, they didn't want to "act white" (see Fordham and Ogbu 1985). Many years ago I developed a series of games that can introduce and reinforce literacy through highly motivational exercises incorporating popular lyric music (Baugh 1981). During my early years of interviewing I would routinely introduce topics related to the role of music in African American culture, which in my experience was cherished by all African Americans, allowing of course for differences in musical tastes.

Black students are similar to all American students in the sense that popular music plays a major role in their lives. Music also represented a source of rebellion, as politicians tried to censor lyrics of "gangsta rappas" who glamorized various acts of urban violence, including crimes against women, property, and the police. Record companies were conspicuously complicit in these trends, as they profited from escalating sales of their productions that earned the coveted "parental advisory" label; a label that merely alerts buyers to the profane linguistic content of the lyrics.

I mention music with "parental advisories" at the outset, because their lyrics are unsuitable for schools, churches, and community-based organizations; however, we have found that some incarcerated populations respond more favorably to Lyric Shuffle with music that would be considered taboo outside of jails and prisons. Be that as it may, and acknowledging that the rehabilitation of convicted criminals also demands increased literacy, we turn now to matters of motivation, because many inner-city students are, frankly, bored by traditional reading materials.

All successful students are motivated, and many unsuccessful students are unmotivated; there are no obvious racial correlates to this fact. However, many successful students are economically endowed in ways that the vast majority of minority students are not, and it is this economic inequality, reinforced by educational inequality, that separates the rhetoric of equal opportunity from the social reality of unequal access to quality schools (Carnoy 1994).

Lyric Shuffle repackages an old idea that was used to teach poor white immigrants to read, namely, "follow the bouncing ball." Readers who are old enough may recall that in movies prior to the onset of television (an era when local movie theaters thrived as the only public venue where motion pictures could be seen) it was common to find short features that would call upon the audience to sing along with lyrics displayed on the screen. Many theaters would provide an accompanist for this purpose, a practice that was quite common prior to the production of talkies. Once sound was incorporated with films, the "follow the bouncing ball," sing-along format was pervasive; it served an important educational function as well, because immigrants who wanted to learn English used these sing-alongs to practice their oral and reading skills.

From a purely theoretical point of view we are describing the transition from orality to literacy that all competent readers and writers traverse. I view such learning as lifelong, although prevailing linguistic theories describe primary child language acquisition in oral terms that extend from birth through early adolescence (with considerable scholarly disagreement regarding age-appropriate behavior). Regardless of theoretical orientation, one of Chomsky's (1965) fundamental contributions to linguistic science acknowledges the universal characteristic that all normal children *acquire* language without the aid of formal instruction.

The essential point in the present chapter extends that edict by recognizing another universal—namely, in all speech communities that are also supported by a literary tradition (i.e., a spoken language that is also represented symbolically through an established, institutionalized writing system), all normal children are taught how to read and write. Moreover, the critical transition from *orality* to *literacy* requires formal instruction, thereby accentuating cognitive differences between primary oral acquisition of a spoken language and differential access to the formal instruction required to become literate (i.e., to obtain fluency within and beyond speech so as to include the production and decoding of the prevailing written standard dialect(s) of the language in question). The social universal that, most regrettably, corresponds to this trend lies in the realm of sociology and economics, because access to the best formal instructional opportunities are reserved for the wealthy, many of whom have come to equate their riches with an inflated sense of their intellectual potential.

Your personal interpretation of these matters may depend substantially on issues of linguistic relativity. To which linguistic group do you belong? Did you acquire standard English natively, or nonstandard English, or is English not your mother tongue? Depending on how you answer the preceding question, you may come to view the following suggestions quite differently. As an African American linguist I am especially sensitive to the language demands associated with professional discourse, particularly as they affect future prospects of students who are not fluent speakers/writers of standard English. But I am equally aware that many young minority students value their vernacular dialects, including languages other than English. And many come to equate the acquisition of literacy with two negative characteristics: an abandonment of their native linguistic identity and an abhorrence of any behavior that could be considered "acting white" (Fordham and Ogbu, 1985).

Lyric Shuffle overcomes these barriers. By diverting and converting students' energy through tapping their desire to hear the music they enjoy, we offer motivational reading material that they tend to know well (i.e., music that they otherwise listen to when they are not in school). When students help to select lyrics as reading material themselves, they are far more likely to attend to reading tasks, and every teacher knows that "on-task time" directly correlates with greater prospects for student success.

I based my original formulation on another important linguistic observation: many popular African American musicians and musical groups use standard English in their lyrics. Inflected forms tend to be present, subject–verb agreement is high, etc. As such, these materials can be used to introduce standard English without the corresponding stigma of texts that many African Americans directly associate with the dominant culture.

Lyric Shuffle and the corresponding low-technology games are offered here to anyone who wants to introduce or reinforce literacy with any student who enjoys lyric music (i.e., nearly all of them). I also recognize considerable educational value via "follow the bouncing ball" techniques because they build on established oral linguistic knowledge in direct association with corresponding written representations of texts that, in many cases, are already committed to the short- or long-term memory of (potential) readers.

What follows, then, are brief descriptions of several games that are intended to make reading fun, which is why students are encouraged to select the music. Once suitable lyrics are chosen, the first task requires complete transcription (with the exception of commercial music that already provides a copy of the lyrics). Once a written text of the lyrics is available, games that are compatible with the skill level of each student will need to be determined (i.e., from novice to advanced readers). Again, the music is intended to be motivational for students, and reading instructors who adopt these procedures may need to suspend any judgment (beyond lyrical content) about the quality of a student's preference.

All of the games outlined here should be monitored and supervised under the direction of a teacher (or some other instructional leader). Students should be provided with copies of the lyrics, although some students may be able to transcribe lyrics, thereby producing their own copy. The song is then played to the students, as the teacher/supervisor simulates a "follow the bouncing ball" format, say, by using an overhead projector or a similar device. Once the song has been played, students are provided with (or write their own) word lists consisting of the vocabulary from the corresponding lyrics. Flash cards showing the words can also be used. Any words repeated in the lyrics should appear only once on the word lists or word cards. These lists and cards serve to build and reinforce word recognition and vocabulary.

Every Lyric Shuffle game has a basic format that requires student game players to rearrange the words from the song to form new sentences, new poems or lyrics, or an original short story. Therefore, depending on the reading ability of each student, the task can be adjusted to fit the needs of individual students. As students gain proficiency, the complexity of the games should be increased to present new challenges, and more importantly, to advance literacy.

Unlike teaching aids that segregate reading from writing, Lyric Shuffle bridges this gap by combining elements of both into each game. This integration can be used with a variety of games that can be played by individual students as well as small teams of three or four student players in a contest format. Indeed, Lyric Shuffle contests can serve to motivate students to perform at a higher academic level, and team play can use peer-group support as another means of motivation.

In general terms, then, student tasks involve the manipulation of vocabulary derived from the lyrics to form new sentences or stories, which are directly tied to the relevant song. Again, these games can be adapted to fit lyrics for music from any era, in many written languages. However, the success of this enterprise lies fundamentally in the high degree of motivation that students receive by helping to select lyrics they enjoy. When lyrics are imposed in a top-down manner they have much of the same stigma as do traditional reading materials.

Several teachers have written to me regarding their own modifications of Lyric Shuffle, which they have adapted to meet the needs of their students. For example, some students may request a song in a language other than English, and teachers have used that text as a basis for translation exercises for those students; again, Students for whom English is a second language (ESL) are more motivated when they share ownership of relevant pedagogy, and many consider such instruction to be closer to their culture and personal lives.

With modest additional support we have had considerable success through contest formats, where prizes for individuals and team members add yet another incentive for on-task behavior that tends to reduce disruptive student behavior. Through various forms of sponsorship we have been able to award modest prizes, reinforcing "good behavior" and greater literary competence. Because Lyric Shuffle can be used with remedial to advanced students, we have been able to reward every contestant (following a philosophy much like that behind giving awards to all participants in the Special Olympics).

Beyond sentence formation, and basic phonic lessons (described momentarily), teachers and supervisors can also lead useful group discussions about the linguistic content of various lyrics. That is, what "semantic interpretation" do student players bring to the lyrics (i.e., the text)? Under the supervision of a teacher, parent, or literate instructor, lyrics can be discussed with respect to a variety of linguistic observations. Specific words can be analyzed for their spelling and pronunciation, and meanings associated with particular words or phrases can also be evaluated. Through general discussions of the lyrics as text, instructors have yet another vehicle to introduce student players to difficult linguistic topics like ambiguity, puns, homonymy, and synonymy, and this can be done without direct reference to the acquisition of dominant literary or linguistic norms.

Students who are new to reading will need to master elementary phonics, that is, the correspondence between sounds and their orthographic representations. Consonants are less ambiguous than vowels in this regard and may be introduced first. Vowels are essential, but it is best to avoid the inherent ambiguity associated with vowel-to-letter correspondences until students have some preliminary understanding of less ambiguous cases (e.g., /b/, /p/, /k/, as opposed to /a/, /e/, and /o/).

The most elementary Lyric Shuffle game consists of students circling specific letters (and recognizable sounds) within words in a song. The instructor can demonstrate how students will circle every /B/ or /b/ that appears in the written lyrics of the song. That exercise in turn would be followed by a discussion of /b/ in unambiguous context (e.g., /b/ in "big" vs. /b/ in "lamb"). While this may seem obvious to readers of this volume, these are the very kinds of inconsistencies that make reading difficult for any student, but even more difficult for students whose native dialect is substantially different from the spoken standard dialect(s).

These early phonic lessons should bridge to the identification of inflected forms, such as plurals, possessives, and past-tense endings. The letter /s/ in the word *sink* has no independent meaning, but in the word *cats* it conveys plurality. Again, these elementary observations are not intended to tax your capacity for tedium, but to make explicit the building blocks of literacy. More advanced students can dissect words more completely, that is, by identifying syllables, prefixes, or other parts of words. Eventually, at the most advanced stages of Lyric Shuffle, student players are required to produce their own writing (or lyrics) in ways that meet traditional writing standards, but this process is achieved gradually with student cooperation.

By providing an entertaining format for students to learn and improve literacy, we hope to counter the legacy of academic difficulty that so many minority students have experienced in the past. No, Lyric Shuffle alone cannot meet this demand, but when one considers that music is constantly being created, we can readily see the benefit of including ever-changing reading materials that have a relatively short shelf life in comparison with traditional texts that are intended to last several years.

Also, Lyric Shuffle need not be limited to schools. Parents, church leaders, members of community-based organizations, etc., can supplement traditional literacy programs at school with these games as further enrichment. As long as *What Works* does not work for inner-city students (and other nontraditional students), Lyric Shuffle and other low-technology, low-cost solutions may offer vital intellectual lifelines for less fortunate students at critical stages of their academic and linguistic development.

AN OUTLINE OF LYRIC SHUFFLE GAMES

For the sake of brevity and illustration, some general principles for four different games appear below. At this stage of discussion we are less concerned with explicit rules or point scoring; rather, a series of games are outlined that can and should be modified by instructors and/or the players themselves. As suggested, the games can be adapted to the needs of student players from the three designated linguistic backgrounds: native speakers of standard English, native speakers of nonstandard English, and those for whom English is not native.

The following games presume mastery of basic phonic skills; student players who have not yet mastered phonics should continue to use a format of circling phonemes, words, and parts of words until they begin to "crack the code." Since Lyric Shuffle draws on oral linguistic knowledge, as well as the popularity of the lyrics and texts with game players, the "follow the bouncing ball" format taps into existing linguistic knowledge, which is another clear advantage over texts that are unfamiliar to student players.

It would be impossible for me to predict or designate which game is best suited to either elementary or advanced student players; this decision will ultimately depend on the individual players and their respective skills. Rather, I will outline the simplest games first and gradually introduce more complicated versions. The final decision to play one version as opposed to another can, of course, be modified based on actual player performance. What follows, then, are some simple instructions for how one would complete a series of games. In some instances it will be useful to specify distinctions between individual and team performance, but for the most part these games are designed to be played with a balance of individual and team play.

Game 1: Sentence Shuffle

Sentence Shuffle can be played by individuals or teams of up to four players. The basic game requires that players roll dice to determine the number of words that will appear in the sentence that they are about to create. They then create a new sentence, using the vocabulary from the lyrics and the number of words that appeared on the dice. Points will be applied or subtracted, depending on the roll of the dice.

Students, either as individuals or as rotating members of teams, roll the dice twice to determine the number of words per sentence that the student must create. The student therefore has two options, except when the same number is rolled twice. Points are given based on the number of words in a sentence, with longer sentences receiving more points due to the use of more words. The primary and important exception occurs when students roll "snake eyes"; it is often difficult to construct sentences with only two words. Some teachers offer bonus points whenever students are able to create a two-word sentence. The final score is, of course, based on the accumulation of points for successful completion of the task. As students become more proficient, the task can be timed. Students may keep personal records of their performance on individual score cards.

Game 2: Poet Shuffle

Poet Shuffle is viewed as an individual game, which can optionally be played with dice. The nondice version has no externally imposed restriction on the length of sentences, or on the length of the poem.

The lyrics provide the vocabulary inventory, but students can use those words more freely when they roll dice. In either version, the player determines how many lines will appear in a new poem (or new lyrics). Since poetry requires greater writing skills, players could have the option to use the corresponding vocabulary without the quantitative restrictions that are imposed when they roll dice.

Advanced students should be encouraged to be creative with available prefixes and suffixes as well. As with Game 1, students can compete within specific time frames, thereby structuring the game to suit classroom requirements.

Game 3: Song Shuffle

Students should have a folder or some means of keeping their lyric sheets and word lists together. As new songs are accumulated, additional games can be created that utilize aspects of Games 1 and 2, using additional words from more than one song. In this instance, the individual or team rolls the dice, say two or three times, to determine which songs are to be combined. Thus if each song sheet is numbered, students can reproduce Games 1 and 2 employing the vocabulary of more than one song. The complexity of this kind of vocabulary mixing can be managed as long as each individual song is assigned a number so that it can be randomly selected by rolls of the dice. Scoring would be similar to that for Games 1 and 2.

Game 4: Grammar Roulette

Grammar Roulette would be reserved for advanced students, and would require some mechanism for random number selection (e.g., dice, a spinning wheel, drawing from a deck of cards, etc.). Different grammatical categories would be assigned a number; for example, nouns = 1, verbs = 2, adjectives = 3, prepositions = 4, adverbs = 5, pronouns = 6, etc. The preceding six categories illustrate the point, because a student could roll a die to determine which grammatical category should be identified within the lyrics of the original song, or in the sentences or stories they originally created. In much the same manner that we have converted "follow the bouncing ball," we offer this attractive alternative to various forms of "sentence diagrams."

As students become more skilled, the complexity of grammatical categories can increase and different scores may be associated with the relative frequency with which alternative forms are likely to appear in a text. Grammar roulette can also be combined with Story Shuffle, described next, where—in addition to writing a story—teams or individual players may also identify the corresponding grammatical categories for some (or all) of the various texts they produce.

Game 5: Story Shuffle

When Lyric Shuffle is adopted for classroom use, each game can be played by both individuals and teams. As envisioned, this would be among the final assignments for students at all levels (i.e., elementary/remedial, intermediate, and advanced). Players could use all the vocabulary available from the songs in hand. Thus, if Story Shuffle is played with four songs, the vocabulary will be more restricted than if the same game is played with twelve songs. Teams and individual players are required to write a short story based on the words that are available, without restrictions regarding sentence length, etc. Thus, Story Shuffle represents a specialized composition assignment, but the scope of the assignment is determined by the popular music that the students enjoy.

Beyond the content of these games lie other, more foreboding educational considerations. In this chapter instructional alternatives are offered that have been helpful to some educators who have expanded literacy skills among African American students from low-income backgrounds. However, the necessity for this kind of culturally adaptive educational innovation stems from fundamental disparities in public education that cannot be denied. More specifically, there is a need to reduce and eliminate prospects for professional negligence in educational contexts, and we now turn to these broader policy issues.

5 Educational Malpractice and the Ebonics Controversy

In contrast to minimal standards, standards of excellence are never fully met; rather, they are the engines for ongoing growth and improvement within all schools and school systems.

—Linda Darling-Hammond

This chapter opens with some brief personal remarks, spanning my life in a family of public educators through more recent professional experiences with linguistic, legal, and educational research. It was within the larger interdisciplinary framework of these studies that matters of educational malpractice began to take on greater significance, especially given ongoing efforts to eliminate affirmative action. The Ebonics controversy that attracted global attention early in 1997 serves greatly to amplify concerns regarding African American miseducation (Dewey 1938), because—unlike Oakland's Ebonics venture—many educators now seek to avoid linguistic controversy, particularly pertaining to African American students and their combined legacy of racial discrimination and educational apartheid.

As a child I attended inner-city public schools in Philadelphia and Los Angeles. I was, of course, too young then to realize the potential harmful effects of professional negligence in educational contexts. This discussion focuses on an essential dimension of enhanced educational professionalism; namely, the diminution of educational malpraxis.[1] Although this article is somewhat personal, growing initially from childhood memories as a student in inner-city public schools, and culminating with the Ebonics debate and my recent directorship of a secondary teacher education program, I do not dwell on the vivid episodes of educational malpractice that I have personally observed or that have touched my life in other ways. The scar tissue left by those academic wounds defies objective reflective analyses, even given the passage of time. But it would be wrong to imply that this discussion is somehow isolated from that experience; it is not. It is equally relevant that most of my academic success is due to the persistence of loving and well-educated parents who countered the negative influence of some misguided teachers who did little or nothing to conceal their racial bigotry.

As the son, and grandson, of lifelong public school teachers I routinely overheard discussions at our kitchen table regarding African American vernacular English (AAVE), or Ebonics, and educational malpractice, although they were not stated in these terms. Many members of my family are still teachers in inner-city public schools, where they strive to offer the best possible education against considerable odds. My sister maintains the family teaching tradition; she is an elementary school teacher in a California public school close to the Mexican border, working with language minority students from diverse backgrounds. My uncle teaches at the first elementary school I ever attended, and his wife teaches at another public school in Philadelphia that primarily serves African American students from low-income backgrounds who live in high-rise public-housing apartments. Their experiences—beyond the Ebonics controversy—have also shaped my opinions on this topic, because I seek not to blame dedicated teachers who are committed to the well-being of the most needy students for dismal educational prospects that are beyond their capacity to influence or control; they—like many of their students—are victims of circumstance. These issues were acute when I served as a director of an experimental teacher education program at Stanford University. The vast majority of student teachers who enroll there are white; but, due to rapidly changing population trends, most of their future students (especially in California) are unlikely to be white, and many will not speak standard English.

Smith and O'Day (1991) likewise consider the importance of teacher education, albeit within the more comprehensive paradigm of systemic educational reform, and their efforts have also played a role in this discussion that is perhaps less directly apparent. One present goal, the establishment of minimal educational standards, is no less important than more visible efforts to achieve higher educational standards. In the absence of firm minimal education standards for public education there remains no academic safeguard for the least fortunate students. Similarly, aspirations for high educational standards imply that minimal standards already exist, and this is not consistently the case.

There are several reasons that these essential tasks have either been avoided or ignored, first among them being the utter complexity of incompetence in educational contexts and considerable professional distaste for broaching the subject (Bridges, 1992). Efforts by the National Board of Teaching Standards, for example, are to be commended for setting high national teaching standards, but part of the trend toward enhanced educational professionalism for K–12 teaching and teacher education requires a no-nonsense attempt to prevent educational malpraxis.

Through such a venture American educators can contribute to the national welfare in at least two important ways: (1) Minimum standards for acceptable educational practices can help students (and their parents) identify and avoid educational malpractice. (2) Educators are in a unique position to advance malpractice remedies that minimize litigation.

As an initial point of departure this discussion proposes a fundamental educational standard comparable to that required of physicians; first, inflict no educational harm (see Darling-Hammond 1994). The road to eliminating harmful educational practices is daunting and somewhat treacherous; however, the inherent complexity of educational malpraxis must not deter us from providing all public school students protection from malpractice.

Because American education is socially pervasive and exceptionally diverse, reform efforts suffer from a host of predictable and unpredictable political and economic circumstances within every local educational agency across the country (Elmore and Fuhrman 1993). The bulk of the educational reform literature concentrates on public education, which— after all—is supported through public funding. This thesis considers the role of private education as well, due to vital distinctions in relevant tort law. For example, most public educators are immune from malpractice litigation for a host of reasons—many of which are commendable and designed to shield teachers from wasteful drains of time and financial resources. Unregulated private schools are not immune from malpractice suits in the same manner as are most public schools; there is an explicit or implied contract between private schools and their clients that differs considerably from public schools, which are controlled by local educational regulations, state educational regulations, and federal education regulations.

Difficulties associated with identification of the plaintiff(s) in cases of alleged educational malpractice partially account for the long-standing reluctance of the courts to take strong stands on many educational issues. Also, many educational malpractice cases have focused on teachers (not in-

jured students), where more than one individual has been harmed, or potentially harmed, by wrongful pedagogy that is within the professional pur-
view and control of the teacher. Darling-Hammond (1994) has discussed
many of the relevant issues, focusing on enhanced educational professionalism. Her statements regarding "accountability" in "educational environments that do no harm" are central to the present discussion. So too are
Bridges' (1992) analyses of teacher incompetence, as well as the classroom
case studies that have been developed and refined by the Shulmans (1987,
1994). Based on the preceding research, and that of others, we reiterate the
need for basic minimal educational standards, including standards to ensure
that every school be a place where students are *extremely* unlikely to be
harmed, either academically or physically.

These introductory remarks hint at the complexity and magnitude of this
problem, but educational malpraxis grows from an apparent contradiction
between the fact that all children residing within the United States are obligated to attend school (or show cause for not attending school), without
the benefit of an equally compelling law to demand that they be provided
a "good school" to attend. It is largely for this reason, and the unregulated
nature of private education, that access to quality K–12 education is largely
determined by economic circumstances, although there are obvious linguistic, community, and cultural factors that should also be taken into account (see, among others, Ball 1992, 1995; Baugh 1988; Carnoy, 1994; Cazden et al. 1972; Delpit 1986, 1988; Fordham and Ogbu 1986; Heath 1983;
Heath and McLaughlin 1993; Hoover et al. 1996; Lee 1995; Ogbu 1978,
1992; Tyack and Cuban 1995; Taylor and Payne 1983; Valdés 1996).

Additional remarks include an operational definition of educational
malpractice that has been adapted from medicine, and that standard is applied to illustrative cases that culminate with Ebonics. The evidential review begins with three examples of official intervention before introducing
a series of court cases that illustrate a range of precedents and opinions
regarding educational malpractice.

Efforts to compare medical malpractice to educational malpractice
have additional restrictions, because pediatricians are more akin to teachers
as both care for children who are not legally responsible for their own welfare. The Ebonics controversy focuses narrowly on the linguistic welfare of
African American students, but it provides the basis upon which to consider
combinations of related issues that extend the frames of educational malpraxis to individual students, that is, beyond language. The 1979 "black

English trial" provides the strongest legal precedent regarding Ebonics, along with other educational programs and related court rulings based on race.

TOWARD AN OPERATIONAL DEFINITION
OF ''EDUCATIONAL MALPRACTICE''

> The general rule the courts apply to determine if malpractice has been committed is to ask: Has this doctor [teacher] performed in a manner consistent with his educational level and training, and in a manner consistent with the work of doctors [teachers] of similar education and training in the community? —D. J. Flaster

Here we suggest that substituting "teacher(s)" for "doctor(s)" in the preceding quotation provides an operational definition for professional negligence on the part of teachers. Flaster points out another distinction that is relevant to the discussion at hand:

> A physician is held to a standard of performance representative of accepted professional skills, but not all physicians are held to the same level of performance. A general practitioner is not expected to be as knowledgeable about the fine points of cardiac diagnosis or treatment as the cardiologist who has trained for as many as six additional years in this special field. (Flaster 1983, 2)

He also notes that:

> Two additional elements that are necessary to make a clear case on the basis of this doctrine are
> 1. The "agent" (object) that was the cause of the injury was under the exclusive control of the alleged wrongdoer, i.e., the doctor being sued.
> 2. The injury was not caused by or contributed to by the patient. (Flaster 1983, 29–30)

By making another substitution, namely, that of "student" for "patient" in the preceding quotation, we direct the locus of *educational malpractice* toward individual students, which is more comparable with medical malpractice where injury to individuals is the most common basis of typical malpractice suits.

EVIDENTIAL REVIEW

Proof of *educational malpraxis* exists in many forms. We first identify incontrovertible episodes of educational malpractice that were handled by cognizant educational or political authorities who removed negligent educators. Beyond these extreme examples, that is, where educational authorities intervened to prevent educational wrongdoing, lie cases of educational malpractice that were taken to court—that is, where plaintiffs sued defendant educators seeking financial remuneration or some other manner of educational redress. Several of these cases center on categorical programs, such as special education for students with disabilities, Title I for students who are poor, and Title VII for students who are not native speakers of English.

While these cases help delineate the parameters of educational malpractice, they do not provide a comprehensive profile of educational malpraxis, and neither does the present illustrative survey of the topic. Rather, they have been chosen with our focus on Ebonics in mind; most of the evidential review is either directly or indirectly relevant to the linguistic controversy that grew from the Oakland school board resolutions that declared Ebonics to be the primary home language of twenty-eight thousand African American students within that school district. The three linguistic divisions introduced in Chapter 1 lie at the very heart of the Ebonics controversy, which centers around this question: Is Ebonics a dialect of English, or a language other than English?

Figure 3 doesn't resolve this debate; it identifies a comprehensive model of linguistic diversity in the United States. This, again, includes: (1) native standard English speakers (SE), (2) students for whom standard English is not native (SENN), and (3) students who are eligible for Title VII funding because—for them—English is not native (ENN).

FIGURE 3. Linguistic divisions among U.S. residents based on their native language.

Abbreviation	Residents for whom:
SE	Standard English is native
SENN	Standard English is not native *(Includes all native speakers who are not SE)*
ENN	English is not native

The evidential review concludes with a summary of existing evidence before turning to other malpractice issues that have been discussed at greater length among health care professionals, but which are no less relevant to the educational welfare of K−12 students who attend public schools.

OFFICIAL INTERVENTION

Three episodes illustrate examples of profound educational negligence that required official intervention. Although the courts were engaged in the case of the state takeover of Newark schools in 1995, ultimately it was the responsibility of the state educational commissioner in association with the state board of education to resolve that matter. The second example corresponds to a fraud perpetuated by an urban school superintendent, and the third illustration focuses more specifically on a classroom teacher, and his ill-conceived mode of instruction that was potentially harmful to an entire class of students, most of whom were minority children attending an inner-city school.

Many readers may already know of the May 1995 actions taken by Leo Klagholz, then New Jersey state education commissioner. He submitted a formal recommendation to the New Jersey State Board of Education that elected school board officials in Newark be replaced by a state-appointed school board due to the fact that they "had failed for years to fix a badly broken system." This recommendation eventually found its way into court, at which time Stephen G. Weiss, an administrative law judge, endorsed the state effort to oust the Newark school board. He rebuffed efforts by the school district's attorney, who called for a series of hearings that might have otherwise postponed the board's ouster, observing that the takeover had not been "arbitrary, capricious, or unreasonable."

However, Judge Weiss's ruling was not binding; the ultimate decision fell to the state education commissioner and the New Jersey state board of education. In July 1995 the state board voted to take over the 82 Newark public schools on the basis of dismal test scores, questionable spending practices, high dropout rates, and dilapidated facilities. Again, the pattern of these conditions had existed for several years before state educational officials intervened. This clearly suggests that many cohorts of students who attended Newark schools, as well as teachers who tried to teach under less than optimal conditions, were the victims of either willful or unintentional educational negligence and, perhaps, malfeasance.

This example shows that alleged or potential misconduct by members of a school board can have devastating educational consequences for students from any background (including children who are American slave descendants), their teachers, and parents who rely on those officials to maintain adequate educational facilities and provide academic opportunities that will meet some basic (minimal) standard of professional competence to ensure that the promise of public education is more than a mere farce performed at considerable taxpayer expense.

The second illustration concerns a former superintendent of schools of an urban California school district who perpetuated a long-standing fraud based on misleading credentials that indicated he had received a doctorate in psychology from Stanford University. A meticulous Stanford doctoral student who was serving as an intern within the school district attempted to locate the superintendent's dissertation without success. It was never the intention of the graduate student to bring down the superintendent; she merely wanted to read his dissertation. Unable to locate the document, the student made normal inquiries for further assistance, only to learn that no such dissertation existed, nor had the superintendent ever been enrolled at Stanford.

Initial reports at the time were somewhat murky, in part because the alleged wrongdoer was popular with students, parents, educators, and he had a good reputation among scholars in higher education. However, when this fraud was exposed the school board had no alternative but to terminate his contract. Ensuing investigations revealed additional evidence of wrongdoing, including his pocketing of student funds for personal and entertainment expenses, along with other documented examples of official misconduct. The fraudulent credentials were created years before at a time when the former superintendent was a school principal. He took time off from his regular duties, with the support of his superiors, who believed that he was using that time to complete his graduate studies. Upon the alleged completion of his doctorate, he added this new and impressive credential to his personnel file, which not only increased his salary, but also his professional stature within the school district. His career, based on the fraudulent credentials, advanced until the long-standing professional deceit was accidentally exposed.

The next example of official educational intervention in a case of educational malpractice focuses on the behavior of an individual classroom teacher, and it is particularly informative here because his actions meet all of the defining criteria for malpractice that have been adapted from those for physicians. The incident was reported by the Associated Press, 9 March 1994, as follows. The text has been modified slightly to eliminate specific references to individuals associated with the episode.

Use of Parody Test Costs Teacher His Job

Chicago (AP) 1994. A teacher who gave sixth-graders a math test with questions about pimps, drug dealers, and illicit sex agreed to resign from the Chicago public school system.

The Board of Education attorney said Wednesday that the teacher in question, who was transferred to a desk job away from students last month, will leave Chicago's schools.

"His use of a document—I hate to call it a test—was inappropriate as an instructional tool," stated the attorney.

The so-called exam was a racist parody that had been copied and faxed to schools and offices around the country this spring. It included questions such as these:

- "Hector knocked up six of the girls in his gang. There are 27 girls in the gang. What percentage of the girls in the gang has Hector knocked up?"
- "Martin wants to cut his half-pound of heroin to make 20 percent more profit. How many ounces of cut will he need?"

The teacher, who administered the test, could not be reached for comment.

The test created a furor among parents at an elementary school in a low-income neighborhood, marred by drug activity and crime.

Parents said they felt betrayed because the school is supposed to be the one place where their children are shielded from the storm of the streets.   (Associated Press March 9, 1994)

As far as educational malpractice is concerned, the teacher in question did not perform in a manner consistent with his educational level and training, nor was this test consistent with the work of other teachers of similar education and training in the community. Additional consideration confirms malpractice, and implies potential malfeasance: The teacher in this case was the "agent" who caused psychological and/or emotional injuries, and the relevant instruction was under the exclusive control of the alleged wrongdoer. Also, any resulting injuries or mental anguish were not caused by or contributed to by the students.

Consistent with the orientation of teacher-focused case studies, potential injury in this instance corresponds to a class of students, not merely a single student. But this brings us to another matter regarding the locus of educational malpractice. In medical cases it is the individual patient who may sue as the victim of professional negligence or incompetence. Individual students who are enrolled in public schools are not afforded the same legal recourse; one obvious reason for this paradox lies in the fact that teachers serve "a class" of students simultaneously, whereas the attending physician normally examines one patient at a time. As we shall see momentarily, it is this fundamental difference in the professional-to-client ratio of teachers in contrast to physicians that challenges the essential proof of causality that is required in any successful malpractice litigation. The preceding case differs in the sense that the entire class of students who received the document (the "test") in question were all potential victims of harm—especially in the form of mental anguish.

Each of the preceding illustrations of (alleged) educational malpractice was resolved through official intervention which, for the most part, did not require substantial judicial engagement. They reveal educational malpractice at different levels within educational systems, from school boards to individual classroom teachers. They also represent examples where responsible school officials were presented with evidence of educational malpractice that required their direct intervention. Had the relevant information been concealed from school officials, however, these illustrative examples might not have ever come to light.

It is partially for this reason, namely, that some school authorities simply do not have access to all of the relevant activities within the schools and classrooms under their respective jurisdiction, that some alleged cases of educational malpractice have come to public attention through the courts. Below we review some cases, focusing on their relevance to educational malpraxis and the need to affirm minimal educational standards to ensure all students have access to competent learning environments within the nation's public schools.

ILLUSTRATIVE COURT CASES REGARDING EDUCATIONAL MALPRACTICE

Special Education and the Case of E. J.

The case in question began in 1991 when E. J., the plaintiff, was a first-grade student with adequate-to-superior schoolwork, but he also showed early signs of being "restless and disruptive." After long and contentious court fights a federal appeals court found that the school district "violated the child's rights under two Federal laws guaranteeing special school programs for disabled children, the Individuals With Disabilities Education Act (IDEA) and the Rehabilitation Act of 1973" (Hanley 1996, 18). Similar suits have usually been settled by school districts paying for private schooling, therapy, or other special programs. The difference in this instance is that punitive damages against individual teachers and school officials have been called for. Fiscal pressures and other economic constraints have given education officials considerable pause regarding the prospect of legal expenses for capricious malpractice suits centered on individual students, rather than entire classes. "The district's insurance policy covers compensatory damages but not punitive damages." Beyond the costs of insurance coverage lie matters regarding whether or not individual school officials or teachers shall be indemnified by their school districts—and the taxpayers who fund those districts.

The immediate reaction of education officials has been to seek further federal protection: in an article in the *New York Times,* February 18, 1996, R. Hanley reported that "the school boards association and the American Association of Administrators want Congress to amend the laws to prohibit compensatory and punitive damage awards." While these political steps may be necessary, they are certainly insufficient to remove the underlying causes of educational malpraxis from which the plaintiff was seeking relief.

What, then, of malpractice? Did these educators perform in a manner consistent with their training and that of their professional peers? Perhaps they did. Did these educational "agents" cause injury that was under their exclusive control? Perhaps they did. Did the student, or the student's parents, contribute to the injury? Perhaps they did not.

Unless all three of the above conditions are met as described previously, this case would not meet the operational definition for educational malpractice. More precisely, if the cognizant legal and educational authorities, or a jury, determine that (1) the educators named in the suit did not perform in a manner consistent with their education, training, or that of their peers, and (2) that these educational "agents" caused injuries that were under their exclusive control, and (3) that the students' (or the students' parents) did nothing to contribute to the alleged injury—then, and only then—would this case meet the basic criteria for malpractice litigation.

Donohue v. Copiague Union Free School District

According to Culhane (1992, 387), the case in question "represented the paradigmatic 'functional illiteracy' case, in which a student alleges [*sic*] that the education was deficient in a wholesale way." Essentially, the plaintiff in this case alleged that teachers were negligent and that his educational failure was not due, in any way, to personal shortcomings on his part or that of his parents, but instead were the result of flaws within the defendant school system that did not conform to relevant educational law which stated "that each pupil who continuously failed or who was listed as an 'under-achiever' be evaluated to ascertain the physical, mental and social causes of the under-achievement and to further determine if the pupil might benefit from special educational programs." (Culhane 1992, 389)

The court disallowed the claim on the grounds that teachers are responsible for educating several students simultaneously (as previously mentioned), and differences in students' abilities and educational motivation play a considerable role in the success, or lack thereof, of a teacher's educational objectives and aspirations for their students. "It is simply not realistic to argue that schools 'hold themselves out' as able to deliver graduating classes of students equipped with skills necessary to succeed beyond the classroom." (Culhane 1992, 388).

The courts argued that the "plaintiff's dismal report cards" provided adequate notice to the student's parents of his low academic achievement, and, thus alerted, they were within their rights to request the necessary tests to determine if he qualified for special educational programs or assistance. One judge dissented in this ruling, observing that the defendant school district should have taken the initiative of testing the plaintiff rather than promoting him until he graduated, after which the plaintiff and his parents brought suit against the school district because of his functional illiteracy and its devastating consequences for his diminished employment prospects.

Again, the courts ruled in favor of the defendant school district, but not before alerting educators to the fact that student promotion based on social standing, rather than academic standing, exposed the defendant school district to this litigation in the first place. Culhane (1992, 390) further observes that "the result should be different where the state mandates that certain minimum scores be achieved on periodic tests before the student is permitted to advance to the next grade (or subject) level."

Hoffman v. Board of Education

In this instance a misdiagnosis regarding "plaintiff's abilities (or disabilities) led to a tragic misplacement and resulting injury" (Culhane 1992, 391). The plaintiff had been given an IQ test by a qualified "clinical scientist" who was employed by the defendant school board, and due to a low score (74) the plaintiff was just below the district's cutoff score of seventy-five, thereby indicating that the plaintiff should be placed in a class for "mentally retarded" students.

The clinician who administered the test concluded that the low score was due, in large measure, to speech problems, and a written evaluation was provided suggesting that the plaintiff "needs help with his speech problem in order that he be able to learn to make himself understood. Also his intelligence should be reevaluated within a two-year period so that a more accurate estimation of his abilities can be made" (Culhane 1992, 391).

In short, this was not done; unlike the Donohue case, the parents were not told of their son's score (one point below the cutoff for placement in the special education class), and they were not told of the internal memo that encouraged retesting of the child. Eleven years passed before the child was retested, at which time his IQ was found to be within "the normal range, at ninety-four."

As we shall see from evidence drawn from the next case, known as the "black English trial," it is important to note that the plaintiff in the present case "alleged that defendants had been negligent in testing and subsequently placing him in a class for the mentally retarded, and in refusing to follow adequate procedures for the recommended retesting of plaintiff's IQ. Significantly, the injuries alleged were not of 'functional illiteracy'; rather, plaintiff alleged 'mental anguish' at having been classified as retarded" (Culhane 1992, 391)

This case centers squarely on duties of disclosure by the defendant school district. Unlike comparable cases of medical malpractice between a doctor and an adult patient, the fact that schools and teachers are acting in loco parentis (i.e., they occupy a role similar to that of a parent while children are in their care) adds further to their professional responsibility to disclose information relevant to the educational welfare of individual students.

Concerns regarding student misplacement were central to the black English trial, and will be equally evident as we reconsider the Ebonics controversy along with concerns regarding the placement of students into special programs or classes based on their race rather than through some suitable educational diagnostic.

The Black English Trial Revisited

The black English trial occurred in 1979 and centered around eleven African American students who were diagnosed as being "linguistically handicapped." Much like the Hoffman case, a specialist—in this instance a certified speech pathologist—conducted a series of diagnostic tests that resulted in the plaintiffs' being placed in special education classes that delayed their academic development. Judge Charles Joiner, whose opinion is presented in full elsewhere (Smitherman 1981), ruled in favor of the plaintiffs. He observed that students were being asked to perform using standard English, but the teachers failed to acknowledge their native vernacular dialect (AAVE), which happens not to coincide with the prevailing standard linguistic norms necessary for normal academic development in typical public schools throughout the nation.

The judge's ruling failed to address a concern I have previously discussed at considerable length (Baugh 1988, 1998). Dialectal differences between standard English (i.e., the dialect of the middle and upper classes) and dialects that are not standard (i.e., spoken by the working and lower classes, or by those who are not native speakers of the dominant language[s]) should not be attributed to pathological causes. The linguistic consequences of slavery in the United States are well known to linguists (Bailey and Maynor 1987; Baugh 1983; Chambers 1983; Green 1995; Labov 1972a, 1982; Mufwene 1992; Rickford 1986; Smitherman 1977; Wolfram 1969), and some educators who are mindful of these linguistic differences have devoted themselves to finding suitable educational solutions in support of African American students (Ball 1991, 1992, 1995; Banks 1994; Baugh, B. 1994; Foster 1997; Gee 1990; Hollins, King, and Hayman 1994; Hoover et al. 1996; Ladson-Billings 1995; Lee 1995; Rickford and Rickford 1995). Speech pathologists have also recognized that linguistic diagnostics for African American students require special attention, and much of that recognition grew directly from issues raised during the black English trial (Seymour and Seymour 1981; Stockman and Vaughn-Cooke 1989; Washington and Craig 1994; Wyatt 1995). Much of the relevant research in linguistics, education, and speech pathology was spawned by the black English trial, where educators—relying on test results derived from pathological speech diagnostics—were simply unaware of the relevant linguistic heritage of American slave descendants.

Despite the considerable linguistic evidence that was presented at the time of the trial, Judge Joiner's ruling skirted the educational consequences facing students for whom standard English is not native (SENN), whereas the corresponding law cited in his ruling was adopted by Congress in 1974 specifically to support students for whom English is not native (ENN). As a result of this judicial avoidance, it still remains legal to use pathological diagnostics to place African American students in remedial (or bilingual) classes, which, as we learned from Judge Joiner's ruling, may be detrimental to their educational welfare.

Under these circumstances I argue (Baugh 1998) that many African American students are ill served by linguistic misclassification, owing in large measure to a combination of inadequate linguistic diagnostics and educational policies that dismiss nonstandard English as a barrier to academic success. Some of these policies, and their lack of adequate linguistic dexterity, help to explain racial discrepancies in academic performance on standardized tests (Williams 1975; Steele et al. 1993). What of current practice? Fortunately some speech pathologists have begun to address the fact that the linguistic consequences of slavery and educational apartheid have never been adequately addressed. By "adequate" we mean equal educational opportunities and performances from students regardless of their background (Wolfram 1993; Wyatt 1995, 1996).

There are other problems associated with the linguistic circumstances surrounding African American students who do not speak standard English as it relates to educational malpractice. Teachers who rely on results from pathological speech diagnostics would: (1) be performing in a manner consistent with their training and peers (as did the teachers in the black English case), (2) the cause of any ensuing educational harm is unlikely to be under their exclusive control, and (3) the "cause" of educational injuries resulting from the dual legacy of slavery and a prior history of racialized educational apartheid are clearly not the fault of any living teacher. Therefore, any suggestion that classroom teachers in inner-city schools are causal agents of willful educational malpractice will rarely prove true, but while this may be welcome news to educators in inner-city (and rural) schools that serve large populations of students from low-income and minority backgrounds, it does little to truly improve educational prospects for African American students.

EVIDENTIAL SUMMARY

Thus far we have considered two strands of potential relief from educational malpractice, namely, official intervention and litigation. The examples of official interventions are simultaneously heartening and disturbing; they are laudable in the sense they provide clear evidence where educational wrongdoing has been eliminated "within the system." On the downside, these examples of official intervention do not offer the kind of immediate relief from educational harm that most of us would prefer to see enacted upon confirmation of educational malpractice. Since public schools are also considered to exist for general public welfare, no one who values the importance of an educated citizenry within a democracy that values equal educational opportunities would want to see more, rather than less, litigation associated with effective educational reforms. However, to deny access to the courts to relieve various forms of educational malpractice, albeit in the name of a desideratum, is potentially detrimental to the public educational welfare.

When viewed collectively, the preceding court cases provide a pattern, and although some rulings went in favor of plaintiffs while others favored professional educational defendants, each trial stands as a regrettable testament of wrongful educational practices that parents, students, teachers, and school administrators want to avoid in the future.

The example of the math teacher who used inappropriate problems is perhaps the most apparent instance of educational malpractice, if not malfeasance, which may account for the fact that it never came to trial; rather it is an example of unprofessional conduct by a teacher that called for intervention to protect students from potentially harmful effects. Educators must walk a fine line between their desire to try novel or experimental approaches that may or may not improve educational prospects, especially for students who are most in need of help. They certainly want to avoid potentially harmful practices that could not only retard academic development, but cause students to suffer mental anguish as in the case of ill-chosen examples about pimps, prostitutes, and drug dealers that were introduced in the name of cultural sensitivity.

The special education case of E. J., which did go to trial, raises the prospect that individual teachers or school officials might be prosecuted and asked to pay punitive damages in cases of educational malpractice. The usual resolution, particularly concerning special education cases, is for a defendant school district to pay for private schooling, or therapy, but there tend not to be any provisions for school districts' insurance policies to cover punitive damages. Internal mechanisms operating within the school could "flag" problematic cases long before they result in the kinds of legal violations that could be brought to trial; carefully documented procedures would assist defendant school districts and educators by confirming the steps that had been taken to assist potential plaintiffs.

The case of Donohue v. Copiague Union Free School District, dealing with a classical case of "functional illiteracy," confirms that public educators cannot guarantee that graduates from individual classes or particular schools will necessarily be equipped with the requisite skills to assure their success at the next level of education or in their pursuit of employment. There are so many intervening variables that are beyond the control of educators that to hold them responsible for the success—or lack of it—that their students encounter upon the next phase of their life, be that at the next level in school or in some occupational pursuit, is incompatible with the free-market economic forces that offer no assurance that anyone will be guaranteed academic success or suitable employment upon completion of school, or classroom, requirements.

The remaining illustrations regarding the misdiagnosis of student plaintiffs and their subsequent placement in classes for students with diminished mental capacities have yielded rulings in favor of plaintiffs and should be the source of considerable concern to educators, teachers, and teacher educators. This is all the more important when students, who are minors, are involved because of the schools' special in loco parentis responsibilities. When parents or guardians are forced to rely on the professional evaluations and judgments of educators, or their clinical surrogates, then it is essential that every precaution be taken to ensure the most accurate possible diagnoses.

In the case of Hoffman v. Board the mere fact that the clinician's documented suggestion to retest the plaintiff had been neglected, and that the plaintiff's parents were not informed of this information, put the onus of blame directly on the school district. The black English trial is somewhat more complicated in this regard, because both the speech pathologist who conducted the original linguistic diagnoses, and the teachers who reacted to the vernacular African American speech of the plaintiffs, were acting in a manner consistent with the professional practice of their peers. Thus, they may not have been guilty of either willful or benign educational malpractice, but Judge Joiner's ruling casts significant doubt on the capacity of speech pathologists or educators to diagnose African American SENN students.

THE OAKLAND EBONICS CONTROVERSY

The preceding legal cases find common ground in the controversy that swept the nation after the Oakland school board voted unanimously, on December 18, 1996, to declare Ebonics the official language of twenty-eight thousand African American students who attend public schools in that district. The original resolution, which was supported by a policy statement, claimed that Ebonics "is not a black dialect or any dialect of English." That statement, and others, proved to be so controversial that the board adopted a revised resolution on January 15, 1997, that conceded that Ebonics "is not merely a dialect of English." Ultimately the board decided to abandon Ebonics altogether.

Circumstances surrounding Oakland's Ebonics episode have been so widely reported in the national and global press, with such varying degrees of accuracy, that a full recapitulation of the incident in this chapter is unnecessary. However, matters related to prospects for professional negligence and malpractice are worthy of review, because each of the cases that we have considered thus far culminate in Ebonic relevance. Ebonics was introduced with specific reference to African American students despite the fact that many other students who are not black also speak nonstandard English (although they do so for different sociohistorical reasons). Without drawing specific attention to the relevant linguistic details, some proponents of Ebonics—quite inadvertently—perpetuated uninformed linguistic stereotypes regarding AAVE through overt racial classification.

The designation of the twenty-eight thousand students in Oakland as speakers of Ebonics appears to be based on their race, and not derived from any form of direct linguistic evaluation. The case of Hoffman v. Board then becomes relevant, where test procedures failed to meet the educational needs of an individual student. Imagine, if you will, the potential legal implications confronting a school district that makes sweeping generalizations about the linguistic classification of an entire racial group of students without some form of linguistic evaluation (flawed though such evaluation might be.) I believe it was—at least partially—the lack of any suitable linguistic test or other educational diagnostic that forced Oakland educators to ultimately discard Ebonics; once burned, they stepped back from the public firestorm ignited by their December 18, 1996, resolution.

Similar concerns over linguistic misdiagnosis were relevant in the black English trial during 1979, but defendants in that case had at least conducted traditional speech pathology evaluations before placing students into their respective remedial classes; they did not merely conclude that an African heritage was synonymous with a black English heritage. Oakland's resolution, and the linguistic classifications it contained, were based on racial criteria and were not the product of linguistic diagnostics to distinguish SENN African American students from those who speak standard American English.

Even if Oakland educators were enticed by claims that Ebonics is not English (see Smith 1992, 1997), the ensuing suggestion that all African American students within a school district should be given a uniform linguistic classification, not merely as speakers of Ebonics, but as students for whom English is not native, is wrong-headed despite laudable educational intentions of teaching standard English to SENN students; however, the Ebonics program was not inclusive of all SENN students, but only African American SENN students, and a combination of federal and state educational mandates created the regulatory climate within which Oakland's Ebonics controversy flourished.

Once this issue had captured national attention, Oakland school officials repeatedly exclaimed that they were trying to adhere to the goals embodied in California's statewide educational initiative, under the Standard English Proficiency (SEP) program, to teach African American students standard English. In 1981 California state education officials introduced the SEP program in an effort to provide special linguistic instruction for African American students who would otherwise be excluded from programs specifically designed for other ENN language minority students. Secretary Richard Riley emphatically confirmed this fact on December 24, 1996, when he issued a statement confirming that federal bilingual education would be denied to Oakland's students who spoke black English. He did not use the term Ebonics, and his use of "black English" affirmed his position that African American students speak English, and not a language other than English of whatever name.

There is, of course, good news and bad news contained in the combined federal and state efforts; the good news is that California state educators undertook an important initiative to address the linguistic and educational barriers that have had a detrimental impact on the academic well-being of the vast majority of American slave descendants. The bad news is that the racial designation imposed by the SEP initiative excludes other groups of students who are also SENN, but who are not African American, and there are no specific federal programs for SENN students. In essence, California state educators instituted a well-intended program based on a combination of nonstandard English and de jure racial classification.

The prevailing linguistic evidence, as well as the legal precedent contained in Judge Joiner's ruling in the black English trial, offers some justification for the SEP program for African Americans, but this has more to do with the unique linguistic consequences of slavery (which included pidginization and creolization), as opposed to mere racial classification per se. For example, Colin Powell is an African American, but he is not a direct descendant of American slaves; his personal linguistic history thus differs from that of the vast majority of black Americans who trace our ancestry to former slaves and have suffered the ensuing consequences of racial isolation and long-standing practices of educational apartheid. These practices continue to be the subject of unresolved desegregation cases in various regions of the country.

The Ebonics controversy has made clear the need to find some way to reform education so as to allow educators sufficient flexibility to introduce new experimental programs to enhance standard English proficiency among SENN students, be they African American or from some other racial background, and to be able to do so without fear of malpractice litigation. And although the black English trial criticized the combined efforts of speech clinicians and educators that identified African American plaintiffs in the 1979 case as being "linguistically handicapped," it would seem that Oakland educators, along with the other sixteen school districts that participate in California's SEP program, would concur that their African American students who are SENN are "linguistically disadvantaged" although this disadvantage is more properly viewed as a social handicap that results from prevailing linguistic prejudice against vernacular AAVE and is not a pathological linguistic disability shared by the disproportionately high numbers of African American students who are enrolled in special education classes and bilingual education classes in different locations across the country.[2]

In the final analysis we must ponder the Oakland Ebonics resolutions as they pertain to the present operational definition of educational malpractice: (1) Are teachers who adopt Ebonics for the teaching of standard English performing in a manner that is consistent with their professional training and that of their peers? In this instance their peers may be fellow teachers who teach classes with large numbers of African American SENN students. (2) Are Oakland educators, be they board members who passed the resolution or teachers who implement the corresponding programs, the sole agents of the alleged harmful effects that critics of Ebonics have articulated? (3) Have students or their parents in any way exacerbated the problem; that is, have they perpetuated the use of nonstandard English contrary to the advice and instruction of their teachers who seek to provide them with standard English proficiency?

Because of the political climate that has swirled around this highly emotional topic, politicians from both ends of the political spectrum have been highly critical of Ebonics, its educational proponents, and the SEP program that gave rise to the Oakland programs in the first place. As the other chapters in this volume attest, there has been considerable misunderstanding about AAVE (or Ebonics) among educators, politicians, journalists, and the general public. Nevertheless, the Ebonics episode triggered highly volatile political reactions that ultimately led to its Oakland demise. However, the linguistic issues described throughout this text should not be ignored. Ebonics, in my opinion, has exposed the tip of an educational malpractice iceberg that is largely concealed beneath a sea of bureaucratic avoidance that has failed to overcome linguistic bigotry in schools or society, and—as Orlando Taylor described before the U.S. Senate on January 23, 1997—such matters are not problematic exclusively for African Americans. Other students are victimized by uninformed linguistic stereotypes and other forms of educational malpractice, and it is this larger picture that is worthy of greater attention by policy makers and educational reformers.

PROPOSED CRITERIA FOR EMPIRICAL AND LEGAL VERIFICATION OF MALPRACTICE IN EDUCATIONAL CONTEXTS

In much the same manner that public hospitals and private hospitals are held to similar standards regarding matters of professional negligence, the time may be right to eliminate dual standards for malpractice in public and private schools if this process can be completed without higher insurance costs or greater litigation.

It will be necessary for educators to attend to the following issues in efforts to engage malpractice reform:

1. What are the relevant criteria by which "teacher performance" can best be judged? More specifically, who will determine if "teacher performance" is consistent with their educational level and training, and consistent with the work of teachers of similar education and training in the community (Flaster 1983)?

2. How will educational injuries be determined, and how will the "cause" of those educational injuries be determined?

3. How will we know if students, or their parents or guardians, have contributed to relevant educational injuries?

Doctors typically defer to local medical review boards to advise them regarding matters of professional negligence. Educators might also benefit from similar consultative and advisory groups. The degree of authorization attributed to such groups, or their decisions concerning when to use the "carrot" rather than the "stick" cannot possibly be established here. However, punitive sanctions may be less effective (and less welcome) than alternative therapeutic solutions (which may be most welcome).

SERVICE CAPACITY: CONTROL AND ALLOCATION OF TIME AND MONEY

Prior to the introduction of managed health care there was perhaps no clearer difference between doctors and teachers than their respective control over professional resources, more specifically, regarding allocations of time and money. Yet these allocations, and their relative adequacy, are directly correlated to prospects for educational malpractice. Other differences pertaining to service capacity are due to the fact that doctors typically treat one patient at a time, whereas the typical teacher teaches more than one student at a time.

Figure 4 illustrates the case for both fields, but it fails to capture another important distinction. Some doctors may see few patients in a day, whereas others may see far too many patients per day. Some teachers—many of whom teach in private schools—are allowed to teach small classes; other teachers—many of whom teach in public schools—teach large classes. Are both sets of teachers to be held to the same malpractice standards? At present they are held to different standards since private schools are not shielded from malpractice litigation.

Those of us seeking medical or educational attention would surely prefer service under A1 conditions rather than C3 conditions. There are no clear educational regulations defining "adequate funding" or "adequate time." The challenge that faces concerned educators, and others who believe in the importance of equitable public education, lies in specifying minimum standards of service capacity—including time and money spent—and precise standards for class size, as well as other resources (e.g., materials and supplies, and assistance for teachers).

The decentralized tradition of U.S. education has produced some of the finest and worst schools in the world. Readers are encouraged to reflect upon their own education, with an eye toward the relative adequacy of educational resources. Do you feel they were adequate or inadequate, and why? Of greater importance to the future of education, what shall we do to

FIGURE 4. A comparative model of service capacity based on local "adequate" allocations of time and money.

Time	Funding		
	More than adequate (A)	Adequate (B)	Inadequate (C)
More than adequate (1)	A1	B1	C1
Adequate (2)	A2	B2 *Minimum standard*	C2
Inadequate (3)	A3	B3	C3

TABLE 1. Rank-ordered Differences in
Allocations of Educational Resources

A1	→	Well above the minimum standard
A2	→	Above the minimum standard
B1	→	Slightly above the minimum standard
B2	→	A hypothetical minimum standard
C1	→	Slightly below the minimum standard
A3	→	Slightly below the minimum standard
C2	→	Below the minimum standard
B3	→	Below the minimum standard
C3	→	Well below the minimum standard

ensure that tomorrow's students will attend schools that meet their academic needs? Table 1 proposes a rank ordering of the nine categories in Figure 4, with an acknowledged bias; time is given greater significance than money.

Teachers who teach in schools and classes that are below the proposed minimum standard cannot be expected to perform their jobs as well as teachers who teach under conditions with adequate, or better than adequate, allocations of time and money.[3]

RESOLVING EDUCATIONAL MALPRACTICE
BEYOND THE EBONICS CONTROVERSY

Despite vast sums of money being invested to formulate new national tests for teachers and students, until such time as the majority of African American students are no longer exposed to educational malpractice, educational equality will not be achieved. This is especially true, and all the more urgent, with the elimination of affirmative action. Although the courts have been very reluctant to offer specific educational remedies to help black students overcome past discrimination in schools and society, the courts have—thus far—shown no such reluctance as they dismantle affirmative action.

The Ebonics debate provides an important opportunity to look at the larger picture regarding educational maladies that continue to afflict black students and other SENN students who tend to be poor. Educational malpractice as it relates to African American students thrives in far too many schools, but there is a systematic pattern of official reluctance—in schools, courts, and government—to acknowledge and address the linguistic legacy of slavery and educational apartheid. For to do so would confirm the need to expand equitable remedies, and not diminish them.

The worst possible prospect for drawing attention to educational malpraxis would be the escalation of legal and insurance costs. The best future prospects lie in the potential for educators to become national leaders in malpractice reform. A combination of legal and fiscal considerations have, thankfully, kept educational malpractice litigation to a minimum, as compared with medical malpractice, legal malpractice, or product liability issues.

The available evidence suggests that "official intervention" may take too long to eliminate sources of educational misconduct, and the courts have been extremely reluctant to offer specific guidance in cases won by plaintiffs who have been victims of educational malpractice. Most judges ask cognizant educational authorities to submit formal plans to their courts indicating how the educational wrongdoing will be eliminated, thereby forcing plaintiffs and educational defendants to negotiate and agree upon suitable forms of future educational relief.

As the child of dedicated African American educators, I know all too well that teachers are often blamed for educational problems that are beyond their capacity to control or repair, and it is with the utmost respect for conscientious educators that I would hope that teachers would be given leading roles in finding solutions to eliminating potential or real sources of malpractice in their midst. More top-down mandates, from the federal government, state government, or local governments, are unlikely to be as successful as would grassroots efforts by teachers who are enlisted in support of this cause. Physicians who are accused of malpractice usually answer to local review boards composed of their peers, who then determine appropriate next steps regarding allegations of professional neglect, incompetence, or misconduct. Educators could benefit from similar models, that is, in contrast to the current external intervention which is often contentious. The essential point is focused on greater teacher involvement in the eradication of educational malpractice.

I have written this chapter due largely to the long-standing discrepancies between poor schools and wealthy schools I have observed throughout my life, beginning with my own education in urban schools in Philadelphia and Los Angeles. That experience has been compounded by that of many of my relatives, all dedicated African American educators who typically teach students who live in poverty in under-funded, over-crowded inner-city schools. Their professional circumstances are extremely difficult, and I believe they possess the knowledge—but not the resources—to offer greatly improved educational prospects to the less fortunate students they teach day-in and day-out. Having known them and their colleagues for most of my life I have always respected how much they have been able to accomplish with so few resources.[4]

It is with this personal history in mind that I believe educators have the knowledge and skill to reduce and eliminate educational malpraxis through reforms that could be the envy of other professions, and welcomed by all; that is, other than the cynical few who would seek to profit from the prospect of greater public expenses squandered on malpractice insurance and related litigation. Such funding, were it available, would better serve the unfulfilled national quest for educational equality.

Linguistic Discrimination and American Justice

Peace between races is not to be secured by degrading one race and exalting another, by giving power to one race and withholding it from another, but by maintaining a state of equal justice between all classes.

—Frederick Douglass, in reply to President Johnson, 1865

Educational quality and judicial equality are closely intertwined, and they share striking linguistic correlations: those who are most highly educated tend to be fluent standard English (SE) speakers, and those who have used the judicial system to their personal advantage tend to speak SE as well. This bias in favor of those who speak with the national mainstream dialect (or their regional standard dialect) in schools and the courts may be understandable, but the sociolinguistic pressures on linguistically disenfranchised groups are not yet well understood by professional educators, jurists, or politicians.

Let us assume for the moment that all children are loyal to their native vernacular, while schools simultaneously advocate mastery of the standard dialect, as they must. The very linguistic allegiance that enhances educational prospects for native standard speakers stands in opposition to the success of nonstandard speakers. While educators recognize the vital role of SE to future success, the demands in out-of-school contexts may be quite different. Most of my childhood black peers were openly hostile to SE, and boys who chose to speak the standard were usually called "sissies" or worse. SE was held in low regard, and those students who rejected black speech in favor of the standard were accused of being Uncle Toms.

By contrast, what is rewarded by teachers—who must advocate the standard—is often equated with so-called white behavior, which can be perceived as a rejection of the native minority culture. Minority students therefore receive mixed signals regarding the power of language, and unless educators are sensitive to this fact, their nontraditional students will continue to suffer the consequences of an inferior education.

Ogbu's (1978, 1992) distinction between "autonomous" and "caste-like" minorities is relevant to this point. Autonomous minorities, such as the Mormons or Jews, are no longer "economically or politically subordinated and exploited by the dominant group." Members of castelike minorities, which tend to be nonwhite, continue to be socially dispossessed, and linguistic differences only serve to reinforce this impoverished isolation.

Members of autonomous minorities have come to master SE as their political and economic power has grown, whereas very few members of castelike minorities have achieved social and linguistic parity. In other words the melting pot is largely myth. The linguistic dimension of this melting, or lack of it, has racist roots. Although autonomous minorities are still subject to prejudice, their social standing tends to be equal to or better than that of other whites who typically compose immigrant minorities. Nonwhite minorities have always been the victims of open discrimination, which makes the task of social assimilation that much more difficult. The linguistic irony stems from the implication that one can somehow overcome the history of racial discrimination through a good education and mastery of SE, although the very adoption of SE may be considered a rejection of the native vernacular and its people.

THE SITUATIONAL DIMENSION OF LINGUISTIC PRESTIGE

My previous research on African American vernacular English (AAVE) demonstrates a pragmatic response to the preceding paradox; adult AAVE speakers shift linguistic styles depending on the circumstances (Baugh 1983). Although style shifting is common everywhere, nonstandard speakers exhibit a greater degree of linguistic variation compared with standard speakers. Some of my informants were able to master SE so competently that listeners from different social backgrounds judged their recorded speech to be "white." Other informants would shift toward the standard in formal situations, but strong traces of their nonstandard vernacular were preserved, so that they were judged to be black regardless of the formality of their speech.

I introduced four situational types into my analyses to determine the extent to which adult black informants would alter their speaking styles based on their interlocutors and the social circumstances. These situational types apply to language usage in different social contexts:

> *Type 1* depicts speech events with familiar participants, all of whom are natives of the black vernacular culture. They also share long-term relationships which tend to be close-knit and self-supporting.

> *Type 2* represents speech events where participants are not well acquainted but are members of the black vernacular culture.

> *Type 3* indicates speech events where participants are well acquainted but AAVE is not shared; solidarity may or may not exist between any two or more individuals.

> *Type 4* corresponds to speech events where participants are not familiar with each other and AAVE is not common to all.

The home environment is typically a Type 1 speech event unless outsiders are present. The school environment is most typically represented by Type 3 speech events, with occasions where all other types occur. For example, if a brother and sister meet for lunch in a school cafeteria, their speech would constitute a Type 1 speech event, despite their presence at school. If the teacher met with their parents at their home, that would be a Type 3 or Type 4 speech event; after she or he left, their speech would again reflect Type 1.

The technical aspects of relevant linguistic research demonstrate the linguistic dexterity of black adults. Children tend not to develop style shifting until they find some personal value in standard English.

This type of linguistic loyalty perpetuates the vibrancy of working-class vernacular dialects in countless speech communities in other advanced industrial societies. Linguistic elasticity is common among members of castelike minorities, who are obliged to make linguistic accommodation. There are pragmatic reasons for this because dispossessed minorities do not have the necessary political influence to demand equal treatment of themselves or their distinctive accents. This can, of course, change through time.

For example, the adoption of French as a second official language in Canada came as a result of pressure from French Canadians. Until sufficient political power is gained, however, castelike minorities will either conform to the prevailing dominant linguistic norms, or continue to suffer the perennial effects of social isolation and discrimination. It is under these less favorable conditions that the nonstandard vernacular preserves a degree of covert prestige through linguistic loyalty.

FORMS OF LINGUISTIC DISCRIMINATION

Linguistic discrimination is an ancient artifact of social evolution, yielding the contemporary mosaic of speech communities that have survived throughout humanity. When discrimination is conveyed through language in spoken or written "discourse," it may take different forms, as illustrated in Figure 5.

These four discourse types distinguish overtly discriminatory behaviors from those that are benign, in the sense that some speakers are unaware of the discriminatory content of their discourse. Type A represents the most overt form of discrimination, where discussants are emphatically aware of prejudicial intent and do nothing to conceal their discriminatory objectives. The Ku Klux Klan and neoNazis are illustrative. Type B is more devious, in the sense that speakers (or authors) are keenly aware of discriminatory intent, but they seek to conceal this fact through some form of deception. Type C represents cases of "innocent mistakes" where some speakers are simply unaware of the overt discriminatory content of their discourse; such statements as "blacks are natural athletes and good dancers" would be a typical faux pas. Type D constitutes communicative events where speakers unknowingly convey discriminatory remarks, but they do so in a mitigated

FIGURE 5.   Discourse types for identifying linguistic discrimination.

	Overt discrimination	Covert discrimination
Aware of discrimination	Type A	Type B
Unaware of discrimination	Type C	Type D

manner. News broadcasts often contain such comments, where reporters unknowingly make discriminatory statements, but do so indirectly.

LANGUAGE CONTACT AND CORRESPONDING PREJUDICE

Weinreich (1953) is sensitive to issues of linguistic prejudice, and it is no accident that many of the examples he identifies are relevant to speech communities where linguistic discrimination has accompanied language contact. His work affirms another fundamental principle of linguistic science: all dialects and languages are equal from a theoretical point of view. Linguistic discrimination defies that egalitarian principle, however, because most people maintain strong linguistic loyalties and values, which come to define those languages and dialects they cherish, as well as those they abhor. Several capricious factors, such as linguistic elitism, reinforce discrimination; people who harbor inflated senses of linguistic self-worth are all too often intolerant of those they consider to be linguistically inferior (Pinker, 1994).

Linguistic discrimination is inherently social, and evidence from culturally diverse speech communities suggests that language barriers are usually the product of social boundaries between groups (Manes and Wolfson 1985). To the extent that one or more groups in linguistic contact perceive themselves as being in an adversarial or hostile relationship, language differences may give agency to discriminatory behavior.

Although discrimination is relevant to several studies by Fishman and Labov, Weinreich's students emphasized different theoretical orientations in their work. Fishman's (1972a,b) systematic development of *The Sociology of Language* is instrumental to a full understanding of discriminatory discourse, because language and the maintenance of social boundaries are intertwined. Fishman (1991) continues to call for the rigorous inclusion of sociological theory within linguistic inquiry, but many socially based studies of language have not taken full advantage of advanced sociological research.

Labov's (1963, 1966, 1969a, 1969b, 1972a, 1972b, 1994) analyses of linguistic variation draw less directly upon sociology, but are no less relevant to the role of language-based discrimination. Labov's (1966, 1972b) classical analysis of /r/ variation in New York City department stores demonstrates that speakers within a same-speech community may be more or less aware of stigmatized aspects of their speech, and this awareness reinforces subtle, and not so subtle, parameters within discourse communities throughout the world.

Haugen's (1972) research on the stigmata of bilingualism in the United States and Gal's (1978) observations regarding peasant speech and diminished marriage prospects in Europe complement the sociolinguistic studies mentioned above, but they also focus more specifically on the human tragedy of linguistic discrimination within speech communities. Blom and Gumperz (1972) recounted similar divisions among urban and rural speakers in Norway, and Ferguson's (1959) introduction of "Diglossia" accentuated speakers' acute sensitivities to notions of dialect appropriateness in formal or informal speaking contexts. Again, classical sociolinguistic studies, such as Brown and Gilman's (1960) examination of pronominal variation, and Milroy and Milroy's (1993) work on "life modes and linguistic behavior," reflect the foundations of language variability upon which linguistic discrimination is based. Linguistic variation does not exist in a social vacuum, and negative attitudes and stereotypes are essential components of discriminatory discourse.

BILINGUALISM AND BIDIALECTALISM

My purpose here is to focus on those problems that arise from our linguistic diversity. An important distinction in linguistics is made between bilingualism and bidialectalism. This distinction is useful in examining the treatment of minority communities within the U.S. legal system. Bilingual individuals (e.g., many Hispanics) speak two different languages; bidialectal speakers (e.g., some American blacks) can shift dialects or style within a single language. Let me illustrate these distinctions among some well-known black personalities: Bryant Gumbel speaks standard English, Richard Pryor is a bidialectal speaker, and the young Louis Armstrong and Joe Frazier spoke nonstandard black English. Among bilingual speakers there are few shared linguistic characteristics; among bidialectal speakers there are more similarities from a linguistic standpoint. The need for translation distinguishes bilingualism from bidialectalism.

Truly bidialectal and bilingual people are at no greater disadvantage, linguistically, in the courts than are other people. Bilingual and bidialectal situations—where a black or Hispanic, for instance, speaks only one dialect or one language and everyone else present speaks another dialect or language—are another matter entirely. In such cases, besides any possible bias grounded in color or ethnicity, a black or Hispanic plaintiff or defendant may face several other obstacles in court: understanding, being understood, and the prejudice of a great many SE speakers toward non-English or nonstandard speakers. This prejudice is the more insidious because it is based on the wholly false assumption that one language or dialect is somehow "better" than another. In fact, many speakers of SE may not be aware that their speech is a dialect too; again, from a linguistic point of view, it is no "better" than another English dialect or than any other language.

Attorneys are usually well aware that clients who speak nonstandard English are at a disadvantage in court, and they will often take the time to coach such clients carefully so that they can make a favorable impression on the judge, jury, press, and other observers. Nevertheless, when speakers do not have a command of SE, they are seldom able fully to overcome perceived linguistic liabilities, especially in a courtroom situation where precise (and standard) English is required.

Bilingual Situations

The case of non-English speakers in the courts is somewhat different. Like every other major national institution, the justice system uses English as an official language; however, given the constant influx of monolingual immigrants from non-English-speaking countries throughout the nation's history, the courts have always been faced with the problem that many citizens, or others involved in court proceedings, may not be competent English speakers. Many of the immigrants who came to the United States never mastered English. Such monolingual immigrants would have been socially isolated but for the fact that ethnic and racial ghettos were islands of cultural and linguistic preservation. This transitional bilingual period distinguishes black Americans from all other groups, because slaves were not transported in coherent linguistic communities. Most immigrants came to America with others who spoke their native tongue. It was the cruel practice of African slave traders to separate speakers of the same language, in the hope of limiting revolts. It was also illegal to teach slaves to read or write. Slaves were linguistically isolated. It is small wonder then that a unique black–American English dialect arose and continues in the vernacular of the slaves' descendants.

Each wave of immigrants has responded pragmatically to the bias toward English in the justice system. Bilingual attorneys have served this special clientele, spontaneously translating both English and legal jargon for their non–English-speaking clients. Unfortunately, the presence of *some* bilingual attorneys masks the need for considerably *more* such attorneys. For a variety of political, economic, and social reasons, neither legislators nor taxpayers (both groups consisting mostly of monolingual English speakers) are likely to support the legislation and the taxes that would enable less fluent naturalized or native speakers to have ready access to bilingual attorneys, judges, or jurors.

The continued influx of non-English-speaking people into the United States will only make this situation worse. In principle, all citizens should have access to equal justice under the law, but this ostrichlike response to the situation of non-English speakers means that many minority people are assigned to court-appointed attorneys who do not speak their native language. If attorneys cannot communicate with their clients, justice cannot possibly be served. However, if population forecasts are correct, we can expect to find more non-English-speaking litigants in the future. In order to anticipate this problem, it may be helpful to conduct special seminars for judges, jurors, and others who will be called upon to participate in judicial rulings. This may prove helpful in the short term, and could be a major improvement over the existing capricious practices in various states and municipalities.

Bidialectal Situations

The situation of nonstandard English speakers is perhaps more complex, partly because SE speakers are often not aware of their bias against nonstandard dialects, but also because nonstandard dialects can span a broad linguistic continuum. The African American speech community is a representative case, as illustrated in Figure 6.

African Americans who interact primarily with other black Americans in their living, working, and recreational domains are most likely to speak the nonstandard vernacular, while those blacks with limited or diminishing contact in the vernacular black culture are more likely to use standard speech patterns; these in turn may reflect either regional or national standards. In 1972, J. L. Dillard estimated that 80 percent of black Americans speak only nonstandard English—that is, are not bidialectal. Another 10 percent to 14 percent are bidialectal, and the remainder speak only standard English.[1] These percentages have probably changed little since then.

Quoted in a *New York Times* article (March 15, 1985), William Labov observes that black and white dialects continue to change, independently, suggesting that the continuum illustrated in Figure 6 might in fact be stretching rather than shrinking. In other words, some black Americans are drifting even further from the majority culture rather than moving toward mainstream norms. With the advent of radio and television, many educators and scholars argued that minority groups would move in the linguistic

FIGURE 6.   A model of linguistic diversity among African Americans. Modified from J. Baugh (1983, 128).

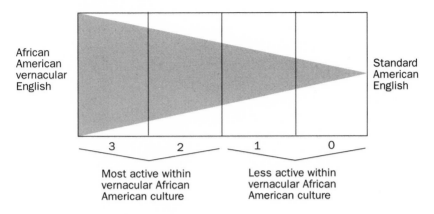

African
American
vernacular
English

Standard
American
English

3   2   1   0

Most active within
vernacular African
American culture

Less active within
vernacular African
American culture

and social direction of the mass media (broadcaster's) dialect. Labov's research suggests that this is not the case. My own work, which concentrates on black adults of all social backgrounds, indicates that there is even greater movement in both directions along this linguistic continuum. As some individuals diverge from the standard, other black speakers are eager to embrace it as they strive for improved education and broader social acceptance by nonblacks.

This point is critical in the wake of Labov's observations because many readers who are unfamiliar with the diversity of black American culture might falsely assume that his research applies to the majority of black Americans. The total picture of the bidialectal black community suggests a far more complex situation than does the process of independent linguistic change that Labov has exposed. His studies concentrate on those black Philadelphians who are socially and linguistically isolated from white speakers. However, it is important to note that this population proves that the mass media has very little to do with how people speak. While these individuals have no trouble whatsoever in comprehending standard English, they do not reproduce it in their own speech.

These complexities carry over to the legal system, as well as to other social and political institutions. When judged by nonblacks, those blacks who speak more standardized dialects tend to be perceived as having a better education and to be more reliable, and therefore more believable. Those who have not had adequate opportunities, or for that matter the personal desire, to master a second dialect are not judged so highly.[2] This is an unfortunate historical consequence of negative stereotypes associated with nonstandard dialects, be they black, Hispanic, Asian, Slavic, or rural white. My professional experience shows dialectal differences to be poor indicators of intellectual ability or personal integrity. Yet the social consequences of racism continue to diminish the potential of those who have not mastered SE, regardless of the reasons for their lack of proficiency.

(NON)STANDARD ENGLISH AND (EQUAL) ACCESS TO THE LAW

For minorities to achieve equal justice under the law, our society must surmount a number of hurdles. The most basic hurdle is economic. Minorities have a long history of being economically disadvantaged. In legal terms, this means that minorities rarely have the opportunity to hire the best available legal counsel for their needs. Similarly, the very demand for court-appointed attorneys at no cost to defendants is a reflection of economic disparity. Only after these economic liabilities are removed will minorities be able to focus on other hurdles to equal justice.

Among these other hurdles are linguistic barriers to equal justice. Institutional inadequacy concerning communication among linguistically diverse citizens within the legal system must eventually be confronted. Just as proponents and detractors of bilingual education seek to resolve these issues in schools, judges and attorneys should do all they can to enhance communication despite the inherent linguistic complexity that derives from the birth of a democratic nation of multilingual immigrants. Only part of the answer lies with bilingual (or even bidialectal) attorneys. Somehow, the linguistic scope of the judicial system must be expanded so that our rich linguistic diversity will not be a liability for any American.

New public policies are warranted in this area. Modest financial commitments to innovative educational programs, on levels ranging from primary schools to adult education, would be an appropriate response to the problem. The ultimate goal would be to make our citizenry more linguistically sophisticated and tolerant. In the bargain, minorities would be more likely to obtain equal justice.

3 PART THREE

Cross-cultural Communication in Social Context

The Politics of
Black Power Handshakes

My thoughts about policies for public institutions that
serve clients from linguistically diverse backgrounds
have been shaped greatly by my mentors. My intellectual debt to Labov and Hymes will be apparent to any
reader who is familiar with their scholarship. Erving
Goffman also influenced my views of sociology, because
my studies tend to focus on the same types of human
interaction that were central to all of his research.

"The Politics of Black Power Handshakes" was the
primary study that I produced under his direct supervision. Its re-publication here is more than mere tribute
to Goffman's substantial influence on this work; it reflects subtle—and not so subtle—cultural boundaries.

The scene is a public swimming pool in a black working-class neighborhood in Los Angeles, on the opening
day of the summer season. The staff members, some
black from the local community and some white from
other communities, are making and re-establishing acquaintances. In a typical reunion, two black staff members greet each other with this dialogue:

Howard: Hey babe, what's happening? It's been a while.
Douglas: Well, you know how it is. Always slow and not enough dough.
Howard: I heard that.

While they talk, Howard and Douglas use the black power hand-shake, which in this neighborhood consists of three separate grasps executed in rapid order.

A white staff member, Dave, then approaches. He lives outside the local community, and neither Howard nor Douglas knows him. They greet him with some hesitation:

Dave: Hi, I'm Dave.
Howard: How you feeling, my man? I'm Howard—and—and this here is Douglas.
Douglas (nodding toward Dave in recognition): What's happening?
Dave: Not much. Tell me, have you guys ever worked here before?

Dave offers his hand to Howard for a black power handshake, with his forearm vertical. But Howard raises his arm with the forearm horizontal, and grasps Dave's hand in the traditional, standard handshake. When they release hands, Dave offers his hand to Douglas at hip level for the standard handshake, which Douglas returns quite naturally.

In American society, as well as throughout many of the world's cultures, the handshake is a display of solidarity and ritualized access in most everyday face-to-face encounters. A handshake takes place after two people acknowledge each other, move close together, and execute a series of verbal and/or gestural cues. Either individual may initiate the handshake.

Like spoken or sign language, a handshake has a meaning transmitted in a clear, defined way, with its own "grammatical" structure. Hand-to-eye gestures, in which one person sees and interprets the offer of a hand by another person, can be articulated and decoded in much the same way as mouth-to-ear utterances. And just as conversation requires knowledge of a common language, handshakes require knowledge of shared norms.

Many black Americans continue to use and develop elaborate new handshakes that demonstrate solidarity under special circumstances. The use of exclusionary handshakes is by no means a radical or new phenomenon. Fraternal organizations have often devised in-group handshakes, some of which are secret. What makes the black power handshake so interesting is that its use has extended well beyond a small group to the point of being politicized.

Athletes use various handshakes and gestures that are highly visible to the public through mass media, but African American handshakes are continually being developed and modified by many blacks. Some whites now use a variety of handshakes as well, serving similar functions to the black power handshake in more intimate circles as a symbol of group cohesiveness.

More difficult than performing an elaborate in-group handshake is knowing when to use it. This decision can place special demands on the participants. At the pool, two old friends, the blacks Howard and Douglas, used the black power handshake as a public display of solidarity and intimacy. But when they met Dave, in a situation in which the criteria of familiarity and racial homogeneity were not met, they used the standard handshake.

During a four-year period, I observed and analyzed more than six hundred handshakes performed at the Los Angeles municipal pool where Howard, Douglas, and Dave worked. (These names are pseudonyms.) At least one participant in each handshake was a resident of the local black community. The exchanges cited earlier were typical of the patterns that developed. In general, insiders greeted each other with the black power handshake and they greeted outsiders with the standard handshake. Yet the decision was not always that cut and dried. Sometimes, deciding which handshake to use demanded quick judgment. For people who actively employed more than one handshake style, each occurrence of this social ritual required a definition of the situation—a decision about which norm satisfied the immediate social requirements.

The use of handshakes between two antagonists, formerly friends, illustrates how involved this decision may be. Richie and TJ, considered to be friendly, had been assigned to seats at the same table at a wedding reception. Yet they were no longer friends. Richie had been dating Diane, but Diane became interested in TJ, whom she began to date on the sly. As is often the case, Richie was one of the last to know about Diane's change of heart. He lost face and subsequently became the subject of mild ridicule. To complicate matters, rivalry between Richie and TJ was not new, since they had been on the same football and track teams in high school. Diane eventually broke off with Richie and began to talk openly about the possibility of marrying TJ.

Eight young black adults, including Richie and TJ, gathered around the table at the wedding reception. All five men, with the exception of the two rivals, exchanged the black power handshake when they greeted each other. When Richie and TJ used the standard handshake with hesitation, and when their smiles turned to solemn, penetrating glances, the other guests became alerted to the antagonism. In the context of the social situation, in which use of the black power handshake was common, exchange of the standard handshake by two persons assumed to be friends indicated that something had gone awry in their relationship. This changing of norms might be the equivalent of one man refusing to shake hands with another man in a white middle-class gathering.

The two examples I have provided illustrate how a choice of handshakes is made in meetings between friends, strangers, and enemies. But what does use of the black power handshake mean in more complex situations involving blacks and whites? Once just an expression of solidarity within black cliques, the black power handshake now serves a much broader population as well. Its use in different situations by white and black staff members at the pool reflects the politicization of the black power handshake and its effect in interracial relations.

Carl was a 22-year-old white lifeguard from outside the community and was fairly well-to-do compared with most of the local blacks. Ronald was a 28-year-old black community aide at the pool. Ronald acted as a mediator between the black users of the pool and the staff of predominantly white lifeguards. Although his job required considerably more physical work than was demanded of a lifeguard, Ronald's salary was much lower than Carl's.

Carl had contacts with people who could provide audio equipment at exceptionally low prices. After news of this "connection" spread by word of mouth, some of the young black men in the local community reluctantly began to approach him about arranging for purchases. At first Carl appeared not to be interested, since he did not want his access to stolen stereo equipment widely publicized, but when Ronald offered to serve as a middle man, Carl agreed. The first test of the arrangement came when Ronald asked for a car stereo for his own use. Expecting used equipment, Ronald was delighted when Carl delivered a brand new unit. Ronald offered the black power handshake to Carl and said, "We got the making of a real good thing here." Carl smiled and nodded in agreement as they shook hands. Ronald then began to distribute the equipment, upping the price so he made a modest profit.

Ronald continued to use the black power handshake when he greeted Carl, once in front of two other black men from the local community who were also interested in the audio equipment. Each of Ronald's friends initiated the black power handshake when they met Carl, presumably as a gesture of good will. Sometimes Ronald invited Carl to stop by his house after work, and Carl accepted at least twice. In all, I observed the two exchanging black power handshakes eight times, generally at a sale of stereo equipment.

From Ronald's point of view, these handshakes helped to maintain good will in the business relationship. Carl, however, could easily have interpreted these gestures of good will as signs of personal friendship. As it turned out, conflicts arose because of Carl's misinterpretation of his relationship with Ronald.

One day Ronald and two of Carl's black customers were lounging with some friends in the shade of a tree on a patch of grass near the pool parking lot, "sipping wine and killing time." Carl nonchalantly approached and asked for a glass of wine. In the group were several men who did not know Carl at all, including one man who recently had been released from county jail, where racial boundaries are not crossed. These men simply did not acknowledge Carl's presence. Ronald and the other customers snubbed Carl as well. Carl then confronted Ronald directly and asked, "What's happening?" The blacks remained silent. Carl then said, "Hey, Ronald, what's happening?"

> Ronald (in a monotone): Ain't nothing happening.
> Carl (turning to another acquaintance named D): Is it okay if I have a sip of your wine?
> D (hesitating): Well, uh, uh, y'see—t'tell—t'tell you the truth, I really don't know—[raising his voice and smiling] besides—it just ain't sanitary and shit to go drinking behind people, specially when you don't know where they been putting their mouths.

The group laughed while they poured wine for each other.

> Ronald: Naw, man—it don't look like we got enough to go round—you know how it is with poor folks, you got to drink it slow and make it last.

The group continued to laugh while Carl, eyes cast downward, turned and walked away. Carl no doubt felt betrayed. In his relationship with Ronald and the other two customers, he had never before encountered the apparent hostility that the group had just directed at him.

From that point forward, Ronald ignored Carl, which only accentuated the difficulties caused by Carl's misplaced familiarity, and which probably added to Carl's sense of being betrayed. Carl's unhappiness carried over into work. Eventually the pool manager called the two in to discuss their bad feeling and the detrimental impact the conflict was having on the other workers. Both men denied that any such problem existed.

> Ronald: Naw, man, me and Carl is *tight,* ain't we?
> Carl: Yeah, we've been friends all summer long. I don't know where you got the idea something was wrong.
> Boss: I got it from the way you two have been acting. Listen, if you're friends or enemies makes no difference to me, but if you're on this job, I don't want to see or feel any tension.
> Ronald: No way, we've been getting along good.
> Carl: Yeah, right.

Ronald rose from his chair and walked over to shake hands with Carl—using the standard handshake.

> Boss: Okay, then, but I don't expect this staff to fall apart. When you're on the job, you work together, because if you can't we'll have to consider some unpleasant alternatives.
> Ronald: You don't got a thing to worry about.
> Boss: Oh, I'm not worried. You can believe that.

The boss turned to his paper work and Ronald and Carl left.

Here, Ronald used the standard handshake for much the same reason that Richie and TJ used it at the wedding reception: the gesture was made in appeasement, to defuse the situation. However, the handshake did not end the misunderstanding. Tensions continued between the two men, and the audio equipment transactions ended.

Although every handshake has its own individuality, owing to the great variety of people greeting each other in many different social situations, there appear to be common forces working on people who have a choice of handshakes to use. Exchange of the black power handshake demonstrates an especially strong personal or circumstantial bond both to the participants themselves and to any observers. Use of the more common standard handshake does not signify such a strong relationship, and the standard handshake is used much less selectively than is the black power handshake.

Allegiance to a group may be confirmed or denied by the use or disuse of a particular handshake, as Carl's experience indicated. Once nonmembers start to use a special handshake, however, the grip loses its potency as a symbol. This is why the politicization of the black power handshake, which has spread well beyond the Afro-American community, has led to the invention of increasingly expressive and ever more elaborate handshakes. In many ways, the development of handshakes is similar to the use of slang words which, as social situations change, are invented, disseminated, dropped from the vernacular, and then rediscovered.

Since few other human rituals provide such highly articulated and observable mutual behavior, the study of handshakes might help us to identify ongoing changes in the norms of various cultures. The existing evidence suggests that handshakes serve important functions in American society. In the community that I studied, the choice of handshakes symbolized and directly affected personal relationships of at least seven people. The indirect effect was probably much greater.

Changing Terms of Self-Reference among American Slave Descendants

Why don't the blacks make up their minds? The whole subject is becoming tiresome. They chose black because they did not like Negro.

— From Valparaiso, Indiana, to Ann Landers, April 1989

This chapter examines the evolution of changing terms of self-reference among American slave descendants (ASD).[1] Data for this discussion are derived from field-work in black communities in Texas and California, a targeted random telephone survey, political pundits, and other minority scholars. The discussion draws on socio-logical studies of changing racial attitudes (Bobo 1983; Fairbaugh and Davis 1988; Sears et al. 1979; and Shu-man et al. 1985) and variable perceptions of racial and ethnographic boundaries.

As one who began to reintroduce the term *African American* before the Reverend Jesse Jackson formally called for this adoption (Baugh 1988), I didn't antici-pate the sudden impact that he would have on this lin-guistic change in progress. During ceremonies in honor of Dr. Martin Luther King, Jr., Jackson stated, "Just as we were called colored, but were not that, and then Negro, but not that, to be called black is just as base-less. Every ethnic group in this country has reference to some cultural base. African Americans have hit that level of maturity" (1988). Pundits jumped at the bait, and a journalistic frenzy ensued; few dialectologists were con-sulted during the media blitz, resulting in predictably false prophecies. For example, in an article entitled "The Power of, and Behind, a Name," published in the *Washington Post,* 7 February 1989, Charles Paul Freund wrote, "If this label sticks, it will be the first time in U.S. history that an ethnic leader has *single-handedly* changed the name commonly applied to his or her group" (emphasis added).

Readers who are familiar with vernacular African American culture (VAAC) will see the obvious flaw in the preceding assertion, because Reverend Jackson did not initiate this dialogue.[2] Bennett discusses the temporal and ethnographic dimensions of this process: "In periods of reaction and extreme stress, black people usually turn inward. They begin to redefine themselves and they begin to argue seriously about names" (1967, 50).[3] Bennett's remarks are reinforced by Rafky (1970), who observes that some black activists and black intellectuals were outspoken advocates of the change from "Negro" to "black" and they viewed this process as an attempt to overcome oppression by rejecting the status quo (i.e., self-identification of ASD as "*Negroes*"): "According to this view [advocated by black activists], the goal of Black Americans should be to assert their pride, raise their racial consciousness, and emphasize their separateness by calling themselves 'Blacks' and 'Afro-Americans'" (30).

DuBois's sage observations provide historical depth to the current terminological controversy. In an exchange published in 1928, which debated the merits of ASD self-reference as "Negroes," he offered a young student, Roland Barton, the following advice:

> Do not at the outset of your career make the all too common error of mistaking names for things. Names are only conventional signs for identifying things. Things are the reality that counts. If a thing is despised, either because of ignorance or because it is despicable, you will not alter matters by changing its name. If men despise Negroes, they will not despise them less if Negroes are called "colored" or "Afro-American." (96–97)

DuBois's statement is obvious to anyone capable of viewing the matter objectively, but there is another issue that shouldn't be overlooked: Who is doing the naming, and why?

Jackson's critics were quick to point out that "colored," "Negro," and "black" are all terms that ASD have used to refer to themselves at one time or another, and to imply that these labels were imposed by outsiders is unfair, even racist. However, Jackson's text is ambiguous on this score; he accuses no one of imposing terminology, but because his comments were

addressed to all Americans, he failed to make critical social and ethnographic distinctions between those who are familiar with VAAC and others
who have little or no contact with ASD. As Freund observes, in his *Washington Post* article cited above,

> The matter seems to have taken some people, both Black and white, by
> surprise; "Black" to them was not a problematic term. Columnist William
> Raspberry, for example, wrote that he "must have been out of the room
> when the question of racial nomenclature came up." (1989)

This element of "surprise" is a reflection of the "Jackson factor,"[4] which
has been evaluated as a questionnaire item in my telephone survey. Did
Americans already know of others who advocated the term "African
American" before Jackson's speech? Results from the telephone survey show
direct correlations between *when* and *where* people first encountered "African American" and their relative personal proximity to VAAC (see Figure
6 in Chapter 6). Most people first heard the term from Jackson, or more
specifically, from news reports about his statement. A majority of this group
assumed that he was entirely responsible for this linguistic adoption.

The following anecdote, from a 1987 group interview with young
African American men from East Austin, Texas (ages 17–26), confirms
Bennett's observation that linguistic conception of this process originates in
vernacular community contexts. In contrast with Jackson's argument, the
Brother takes umbrage at the label "Afro-American."[5]

> We ain't no abbreviated people. It ain't no "Italo-Americans," or "Japo-
> (A)mericans," and they ain't no "Mexo-(A)mericans" neither. We the only
> ones they done abbreviated. That's bullshit! [I hear you.] Black people are
> Africans in America. Ain't nobody from no place else had to deal with slav-
> ery, and that's why they done tried to abbreviate us. But I'll tell you this
> about that. [What's that?] We all came here in chains, baby, but we all
> came from Africa. We got just as much right as anybody else to demand
> dignity and self-respect and that's why I say I'm a African-American! [Other
> men convey verbal and nonverbal approval.]

The Brother makes no reference to "baseless" terms; in fact, he men-
tions black people during his discussion of "African American" (a practice
that I maintain in this text). The preceding illustration is noteworthy, in
part, because it presents another point of view, but also because it proves

that Jackson did not start this process; debates concerning appropriate terminology among ASD continue to spread by word of mouth, as they have since the inception of slavery. Clearly Jackson sensed the changing linguistic tide of self-reference toward "African American," and he used his media visibility to launch this debate into the broader public forum.

VARIABLE TERMS OF SELF-REFERENCE AMONG AMERICAN SLAVE DESCENDANTS

In order to examine this trend I performed some experiments during fieldwork in ASD/VAAC communities in Texas and California. I simply asked people to provide two lists: one that showed terms of respect for ASD and a second list of insulting terms. The questionnaires were delivered verbally or in writing according to consultant preference. All ASD/VAAC consultants were then asked to identify as many words as they could to complete the following sentences:

    1. [Respectful] We should be called _____.
    2. [Disrespectful] We should not be called _____.

Table 2 provides results from 226 ASD/VAAC informants from Texas (primarily Austin) and California (primarily in San Francisco and Oakland).

TABLE 2. Terms of Self-identification among American Slave Descendants

Ages of Group	12–17	18–34	35–55	56+
California	16	26	33	12
Texas	28	36	47	28
TOTAL	44	62	80	40
	R/D[a]	R/D	R/D	R/D
African Americans	32/0	51/3	67/5	22/7
Afro-Americans	41/0	59/3	73/2	38/2
Blacks/black people	44/0	62/0	58/18	18/16
Bloods	11/4	4/9	0/0	0/0
Brothers	18/0	28/0	3/0	0/0
Colored (people)	7/23	4/47	23/39	26/9
Homeboys	5/0	14/0	0/3	0/0
Negroes	9/31	6/49	23/50	27/12
Niggers	0/44	0/62	0/80	0/40
Sisters	8/0	32/0	5/0	2/0

[a]R = respectful; D = disrespectful.

TEMPORAL DIMENSIONS OF CHANGING SELF-REFERENCE

The results are highly variable, reflecting age-graded differences of opinion regarding terms of (dis)respect. Dialectologists will appreciate that this evidence is also representative of an older trend, from long ago when there were no "white" Americans, but only "citizens" (Flexner 1976). "Citizens" were, of course, white men with property; women, native Americans, and slaves were not citizens. However, history has witnessed various pieces of legislation designed to overcome past discrimination and include residents of the United States who were once legally disenfranchised; these laws have been partially successful, as illustrated by emancipation and voting-rights laws. Wilson (1987) provides substantial evidence concerning the long-term factors that have thwarted social prospects for America's latent citizens of color. I also agree with Wilson's observation that racism alone does not account for the complexity of forces that have reduced social opportunities for the truly disadvantaged.

What, then, do these economic, attitudinal, and racial trends have to do with black self-reference? The disproportionate social dislocation of slave descendants is no historical accident; perpetual cycles of poverty and discrimination continue to exacerbate the gap between privileged and underprivileged children, regardless of race. These poverty cycles now touch more whites; as the economy of the United States continues to adjust to a growing reliance on global markets, the majority of citizens—regardless of race—face the prospect that the next generation of children will fare less well than the present one, especially children of single female parents. This (admittedly simplistic) historical sketch of the dynamic interplay of racial tensions and the economy is well established and affirms the legacy of economic subordination that has always plagued African Americans (Wilson 1981, 1987,1996; Bobo 1983).

This background also shows the paradox that linguists face as they try to draw coherent conclusions from the rather dramatic social changes that are taking place in black America. African Americans are in limbo between the best and worst of times—"best" in the sense that more blacks than ever have achieved positions of social prominence, including presidential aspirations. The downside is reflected by changing racial attitudes and growing resentment of affirmative action as preferential treatment for minorities. Political rhetoric has become vacuous, as the liberal ethos of the 1960s is replaced by conservative interpretations for the failure of government intervention to eliminate poverty or racial strife. These trends do not bode well for the truly disadvantaged, who, for many long-standing reasons, are less likely to overcome their legacy of poverty as American economic prospects continue to decline.

It is in this changing social climate that slave descendants have sought to sort out their own identity, and debates over the term *African American* are part of this tradition. Table 2 illustrates the transitional nature of the process; terms that were once considered offensive are now acceptable (e.g., *black*) and terms that previously had polite connotations, to whites and blacks alike, are now highly offensive to a majority of ASD/VAAC (e.g., *colored*). One of my black colleagues observed recently that, even though all blacks may not greet the usage of *African American* with enthusiasm, we all know what we don't like: "Blacks are clear on terms they believe are negative—like *nigger*." Positive terms, however, are another matter. These changes are dynamic and usually take time because they originate within the vernacular culture. Jackson accelerated this process when he thrust the issue before the entire nation.

INSIDER AND OUTSIDER IN PUBLIC AND PRIVATE

In *Hunger of Memory,* Rodriguez (1982) drew an important distinction between public and private language, which, for him in his childhood, corresponded to English and Spanish respectively. Blacks have shared a similar experience, albeit in bidialectical terms, where group (i.e., racial) boundaries often coincide with public and private discourse. The dialect of wider communication (i.e., standard English) is often required in public (Smitherman 1987), whereas private conversations tend to employ the native vernacular, which, for many slave descendants, corresponds to a narrower American population consisting of speakers who have not learned standard English natively (if they have had an opportunity to learn it at all). Figure 7 illustrates these distinctions, drawing on the socially stratified model of AAVE usage that I developed in my study of black street speech (Baugh 1983).

Goffman's (1959, 1972) concepts of "self, teams, situations," and "performance" are instrumental to the four categories illustrated in Figure 7. The private-versus-public division is more or less straightforward. The contrast between insiders versus outsiders to VAAC is more complex, and discussed in greater detail below. Figure 7 recognizes that people use different speech in different situations, especially when socially sensitive language is involved, and terms referring to African Americans fall within the realm of linguistic controversy. Although we are all clear regarding terms that are offensive to blacks, outsiders to VAAC are not concerned with the long-standing dynamic process of defining positive terms for ASD/VAAC.

As suggested above, the "insider–outsider" contrast is variable, based on the dynamic nature of this boundary and misperceptions of where the boundary lies. Figure 8 illustrates this point, denying the implication conveyed in Figure 7 that precise social demarcation is possible or desirable. Such a distinction also avoids racial designation, which has increasingly become a cliché of limited scholarly value or empirical (i.e., biological) accuracy. In Goffman's terms, some people are active performers in VAAC, others are not; this distinction approximates racial grouping but acknowledges the history of racial osmosis that persists within the shaded area in Figure 8.

This boundary also recognizes another fact that has been ignored by many social scientists, to the benefit of blacks who appear white. Sexual encounters across racial lines have been pervasive throughout American history, and especially during slavery when African women in America were denied the dignity of personal sexual choice. I am a product of this truly American heritage. Like many African Americans, I know of blacks with racially ambiguous characteristics who no longer associate with their consanguineous relatives or childhood acquaintances; they were able to succeed where Pygmalion failed, because they have denied their race in order to masquerade as ordinary white folks. Harlem's "Cotton Club" pandered to this trend during the 1920s and 1930s, favoring dancers who were said to be "bright, light, and damn near white." Those who "pass" escape detection because they have, in fact, melted into the pot; these rare individuals are blacks who have denied their past in the hope of economic gain and

FIGURE 7.   Public and private boundaries among insiders and outsiders to vernacular African American culture (VAAC).

	Private discourse	Public discourse
Insiders to vernacular African American culture	1	2
Outsiders to vernacular African American culture	4	3

FIGURE 8. Insiders and outsiders to vernacular African American culture.

Frequent contact ‖ Limited contact ‖ Little/No contact

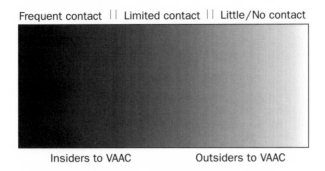

Insiders to VAAC   Outsiders to VAAC

with the desire to escape racial discrimination. Again, the insider–outsider distinction is preferable to racial designations because the latter are increasingly vague when one considers the longevity and complexity of race mixing in America and the fact that so many blacks have successfully passed for white without racial or linguistic detection.

OUTSIDER CONFUSION: IN SEARCH OF ACCEPTABLE TERMINOLOGY

One of the most awkward moments of my academic career happened at a committee meeting, and it is relevant to the discussion at hand. A senior colleague from another department was being introduced to me for the first time; in a failed attempt at humor the stranger asked, "What are you people calling yourselves these days?" I responded, "John. I call myself John." With the advent of time and additional evidence I have a greater appreciation of a genuine problem along race lines; many whites don't know what to call us, which in turn accentuates America's racial abyss. Indeed, terminological uncertainty has haunted many liberals in the wake of Jackson's speech because they don't want to inadvertently offend members of minority groups. Racists continue to use derogatory terminology, with some class (i.e., socioeconomic) implications that parallel private or public usage of racist discourse.

This impression is confirmed by the results of my telephone survey, which was presented as a spoken questionnaire. It was administered to target populations of random households in the San Francisco Bay area. "Targeting" was employed to ensure a representative range of subjects from different social and ethnic groups.[6]

FIGURE 9. Telephone questionnaire with quantitative results.

(N = 205 whites, 62 blacks, 33 Hispanics)

1. Have you ever heard the term "African American"?
   Yes = 248, No = 32

2. (If *yes* for question 1) When did you first hear it?
   (If *no* go to question 3)
   Before RJJ = 97, After = 151

3. Do you think we should not use "African American"?

	Yes	No	No Opinion
Whites	68 (33%)	109 (53%)	28 (14%)
Blacks	46 (74%)	14 (23%)	2 (3%)
Hispanics	16 (48%)	11 (33%)	6 (18%)

4. Why? (In response to any answer for question 3)
5. What terms would you use to show respect to blacks?
6. What is your age?
7. Can you tell me about your family heritage?
8. Do you have a lot of contact with the Black community?
9. Why? (In response to any answer for question 8)

The survey yielded a combination of quantitative and qualitative results. As Figure 9 indicates, the majority of subjects (including several ASD) first learned of the term *African American* from Jackson's efforts. Those who claimed to have heard the term prior to Jackson's comments also reported that they have extensive contact with VAAC. This group includes several whites, such as schoolteachers and shopkeepers who work in ghetto or barrio neighborhoods. Whites with close ties to VAAC, illustrated in the darker regions of Figure 8, tended to report that they had heard *African American* before Jackson's statement. The list of respectful terms (provided in response to question 5, Figure 9) corresponds closely to the terminological variation and age distribution identified among black informants in Figure 9. (See also Fairbaugh and Davis 1988.)

Disrespectful terms were intentionally avoided during the telephone survey. We avoided direct questions about race in favor of self-reports of family histories, which typically provided more accurate details about subjects' diverse racial and ethnic backgrounds.

CHANGING RACIAL ATTITUDES
AND THE JACKSON FACTOR

The qualitative results from the telephone survey confirm some of the positive and negative consequences of changing racial attitudes (Bobo 1983; Shuman et al. 1985; Fairbaugh and Davis 1988). The quantitative results for question 3, Figure 9, illuminate the qualitative responses among those who answered "No." Many, like Ann Landers's exasperated reader, think blacks complain too much; the sentiment that "things are tough all over" was a recurrent theme among most naysayers. An equally strong theme consisted of frequent racial mitigation: "I'm not racist, but" statements are routinely spliced into answers for question 4, Figure 9. Many non-ASD who responded affirmatively to question 3, Figure 9, also denied being racist, although they typically pointed to their support of *African American* as further confirmation of their nonracist philosophy.

One of the most striking sources of potential linguistic tension is reflected by the qualitative perceptions that have evolved among blacks and whites who are racially isolated. African Americans who are insulated from whites also tend to reside in the very areas where the quest for positive terminology originates. Whites who have infrequent contact with blacks harbor misleading stereotypes, and the telephone survey shown in Figure 9 confirms this.

With the racial crossover popularity of rap music, young whites who have little if any direct contact with African Americans are more familiar with terms that are inoffensive (or less offensive) to ASD. These results reinforce the shifting age cohort that Fairbaugh and Davis (1988) have identified as part of changing antiblack attitudes.

Competing perceptions of appropriate terms of respect illustrate potential problems; some whites could, without malice, easily offend blacks or vice versa. Based on the results from Figure 9 and Table 2, it is easy to envision situations quite similar to those I have observed between white home owners and shopkeepers and their African American employees. No disrespect may be intended as reference is loosely made to "Negroes, colored (people)," and "blacks," as if ASD and VAAC also recognize and consider these terms to be interchangeable; Table 2 shows this is not the case.

These results perhaps explain why Jackson's comments provided the spark that ignited a national linguistic debate. For the sake of this discussion it is most important to appreciate the unique catalytic impact that he has

FIGURE 10.   Origin of and change to Africans of slave descent (ASD) terms. RJJ = the Reverend Jesse Jackson.

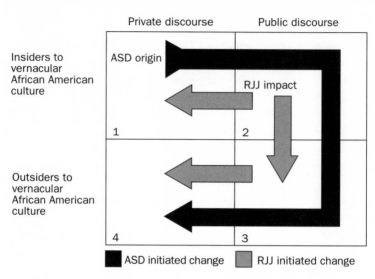

exerted on this linguistic process. Other qualitative results from the telephone survey suggest that, as a controversial public figure, Jackson has developed the political equivalent of a Midas touch, in the sense that everything he advocates becomes politicized, and the waning debate about the usage of *African American* is no exception to that trend, as illustrated by the fact that the overwhelming majority of citizens first heard this term from news reports of Jackson's call to change racial labels.

The linguistic consequences of the Jackson factor are illustrated in Figure 10, where the traditional path of ASD terminological shifts and the more abrupt impact that Jackson exerted on this process are both illustrated. Viewed in purely linguistic terms, there can be no doubt that the trend toward the adoption of *African American* was growing in the ASD/VAAC community before Jackson's comments, and it is in this context that others more qualified than I can evaluate his motives.

Some telephone interviews included comments, volunteered by informants, that pondered these very motives. Cynics argued that Jackson's motivation was selfish and purely political and that he exploited this issue for personal gain. His supporters, many of whom already advocated the change to *African American* prior to his speech, expressed their gratitude that he has the clout to keep ASD/VAAC concerns on the national agenda; they consider this advocacy of *African American* to be a brave and noble venture, and one with considerable political risk. Far from feeling exploited, they are proud of Jackson, and they take solace in the fact that America can no longer ignore their plight now that they have a forceful, eloquent spokesman.

Regardless of his motives, the linguistic impact of Jackson's statement was sudden and pervasive. He shattered the embryonic isoglosses that contained this process within the ASD/VAAC group, a move which, as we all know, was initially hailed as being highly controversial.

CONCLUSION

What, then, can we conclude from these observations? The process that I have been describing is not unique to ASD. Similar processes can be found, for example, among Hispanics throughout the United States, especially those who have suffered similar isolation from the majority culture and the dialect of wider communication. In barrios from California to Manhattan, comparable terminological debates occur among Americans of Hispanic and Latin American descent concerning such terms as *Latino, Chicano, Mexican-American, Puerto Rican,* and *Cuban,* as well as controversial derogatory terms. They, too, are citizens of color who share a legacy of poverty and racial discrimination; they, too, have turned inward in search of their own linguistic and cultural identity (see Le Page and Tabouret-Keller 1985).

From a purely theoretical point of view, contemporary dialectology is the victim of technology, in the sense that mass media can insert new lexical items without prior warning (e.g., Ebonics). Unlike early dialectologists, who recorded data prior to the dissemination of radio or television, contemporary linguists must now be prepared to cope with massive, instant linguistic innovations, often from different languages (e.g., *perestroika* and *glasnost*).

In practical terms, however, these results, which have exposed openly racist verbal confrontations within the academy, point to a potential crisis. Racial conflicts on many American campuses have degenerated into precarious constitutional questions. Do white students have the right, based on their constitutional right of free speech, to mock blacks with racist slurs? Stated another way, are racial insults protected under the First Amendment? This is, regretfully, not merely an exercise in philosophy, because this linguistic crisis remains and has come to a head in different regions of the country, and dialectologists and linguists should be prepared to provide objective insights into this issue.

Today's linguistic paradox is a shadow of long-standing racial and

economic disenfranchisement. To insist on the right to demean less fortunate citizens is, at the very least, the epitome of bad taste. But is it also
willful criminal behavior, akin to a verbal assault? I hope to pursue this line
of inquiry in the future. In the meantime, the Jackson factor looms on the
linguistic (and political) horizon, as Americans from various backgrounds
continue to define, refine, and redefine their own views on how best to
refer to American slave descendants.

4

PART FOUR

Linguistic Dimensions of African American Vernacular English

Steady: Progressive Aspect in African American Vernacular English

This chapter reintroduces the aspectual marker *steady* in African American vernacular English (AAVE; Baugh 1984). *Steady* is a predicate adverb and typically precedes progressive verbs (e.g., He be steady rappin). The discussion concentrates on two main issues: what is the function of *steady*, and how did it come to be used in this way? The data are drawn from two primary sources: natural usage in recorded interviews and responses to a questionnaire. While the orientation here is a synchronic one, a similar usage of *steady* has been observed not only throughout the United States, but in Caribbean varieties of English as well. These attestations, by leading Creole scholars, lend support to the viability of the Creole origin hypothesis for AAVE, although the precise history of *steady* reflects several stages of development. *Steady* represents an excellent example of how the AAVE lexicon preserves unique qualities in the face of overwhelming similarities between AAVE and standard English (SE).

One of the primary reasons that *steady* has not appeared in the existing AAVE literature presumably is that it shares characteristics with SE's *steadily*. *Steady* is what Spears (1982, p. 850) calls a "camouflaged form" and is in this way similar to the AAVE modal *come*. A *camouflaged form* is one that is shared by more than one dialect of a language; however, the form maintains unique grammatical or semantic qualities in each dialect. There may be some overlap with respect to shared functions for these forms, but they must maintain unique characteristics in ways that are not common to all speakers of the same language. In this case there are shared surface distributional similarities with SE, at the same time that *steady* functions as a different aspectual marker in AAVE. Interestingly, users of the camouflaged form do not necessarily realize that their usage differs from the usage of speakers of other dialects. Some informants expressed surprise, and on occasion, disbelief, upon learning that their use of *steady* was unique to AAVE speakers. In fact, one man compared *steady* usage to that of *ain't,* claiming that both blacks and whites used these nonstandard forms, though neither group would use such language in school, or on other formal occasions.

The general syntactic distribution of AAVE *steady* will be presented first. I will then turn to specific grammatical functions, as reflected in unsolicited usage. Evidence will be required to place a few of the examples in their proper ethnographic and pragmatic contexts.

GENERAL SENTENCE STRUCTURE

Each of the sentences illustrated below was recorded during interviews with adult AAVE speakers in Los Angeles or Philadelphia; they are typical examples of *steady* as it is used by AAVE speakers.

1. Ricky Bell be steady steppin in them number nines.
2. And you know we be steady jammin all [of] the Crips.
3. Them fools steady hustlin' everybody they see.
4. Her mouth is steady runnin'.
5. He steady be tellin 'em how to run they lives.
6. All the homeboys be rappin' steady.

The most common syntactic structure can be illustrated by a variable relationship, where *be* is far more common than *is* (see Labov 1969, Wolfram and Fasold 1974):

NP # (be ~ is) # steady # Verb + ing #(#)

Steady also appears in sentence final position, and usually employs heavy stress in this environment, as illustrated in sentence 6 above:

NP   # (be ~ is) # Verb + ing # steady ##.

There are some restrictions on these general sentence structures, and to illustrate these let us examine each constituent sequentially.

The subject of the sentence (i.e., the initial noun phrase—even if it is a pronoun) must be animate and specific. In other words, "A boy, be steady rappin'" is ungrammatical, whereas "Leroi be steady rappin'" is grammatical in AAVE. Some noun phrases using generic *the* are less acceptable with *steady* due to their lack of specificity (e.g., The man be steady taxing everyone). The copula auxiliary form is optional with *steady* in the present tense; past and future are always marked, typically with *was* and *gon(na)* respectively. *Are* was not observed with *steady,* and most AAVE speakers who completed the questionnaire found *are* much less acceptable with *steady*. Habitual distributive *be* proved to be the preferred auxiliary; this is the same AAVE *be* that has been discussed at considerable length by Labov, Cohen, Robins, and Lewis (1968), Wolfram (1969, 1982), Fasold (1972), and Rickford (1975). Full *is* was observed less frequently and was used to refer to present actions as well as some habitual activities. There were no recorded examples of contracted forms of *are* or *is*.[1]

As mentioned before, *steady,* as a predicate adverb, has the specific aspectual function of indicating that the action or process of the progressive verb is completed in an INTENSE, CONSISTENT, and CONTINU-OUS manner. Intensity is the key to understanding the distinction between *steady* and *steadily*. Both adverbs share a 'continuous' interpretation. However, 'calmness' and 'control' are two common implications of SE usage, which contradicts somewhat the fact that AAVE *steady* is always associated with intense activity. AAVE speakers tended to reject sentences that employed adverbs that diminished the intensity of the activity. Thus, sentences like '*They barely be steady rapping,' or '*He hardly be working steady' were disallowed.

The progressive verbs that occur with *steady* are usually associated with habitual or durative activities. Stative and punctual verbs are unacceptable with *steady,* largely because they are not part of a process or activity. Lakoff (1966) and Sag (1973) have examined similar distinctions in SE that are directly relevant to the present remarks. For example, 'He is running down the street' is fine in SE, but '*He is knowing the truth' is not. AAVE speakers employ a similar division with *steady*; 'He be steady running down the street' would be fine, whereas '*He be steady knowing the truth' would be rejected. It is partially due to this shared grammatical distinction between progressive and stative verbs that steady is a camouflaged form; common grammatical restrictions are part of the camouflage.

To summarize: when viewed collectively, these grammatical restrictions specify the range of acceptable usage for *steady*. The subject of the sentence, which is designated by a specific noun or pronoun, must be the animate agent of an action or process. The event can occur in the past or nonpast. Most speakers use *steady* in the nonpast, distinguishing between habitual and present events with the optional use of *be* or *is* respectively. A word of caution is in order, though, because this pattern was not categorical; there were a few instances where speakers clearly used *be* to refer to present events and *is* to describe habitual actions. *Steady,* the aspectual marker, indicates that the activity of the corresponding progressive verb is conducted in an intense, consistent, and continuous manner. It is largely for this reason that static and punctual verbs do not occur with *steady*; they are not active processes.

Because the difference between AAVE *steady* and SE *steadily* is subtle in some environments, and because many readers may be unfamiliar with AAVE, to say nothing of aspectual marking in AAVE, it will be useful to examine some of the recorded examples in their social setting. The grammatical distinctions are much clearer in the pragmatic context of everyday speech.

LINGUISTIC FUNCTION

Three examples should be sufficient to illustrate the aspectual function of *steady* during ordinary conversation. Let us begin with the first example from the preceding section. When the speaker said, "Ricky Bell be steady steppin in them number nines," he was referring to the fact that Bell was an excellent football player. As a halfback he would run in an intense, consistent, and continuous manner. It is, once again, the intensity of the action which is the unique aspectual quality for AAVE.

Another example was produced when I interviewed five adult members of a black family in Los Angeles. The topic of discussion was black intelligence, Arthur Jensen, and the complexity of the human brain. A fifty-four-year-old man, the patriarch, who was originally from Louisiana, was discussing flaws in Jensen's well-known hypothesis about black intelligence. The discussion became heated, primarily because of the controversial and provocative nature of Jensen's position, particularly among black Americans. He argued that Jensen had not conducted sufficient research to justify his position; moreover, he felt that Jensen had taken a simplistic view of black Americans as well as the intricate nature of the human brain. As the gentleman spoke the passion in his voice escalated, and it was in this excited atmosphere that he exclaimed, "And inside of you . . . you've got a mind that's . . . that's . . . see, your mind is steady workin. It's your subconscious mind." The opinions of Jensen notwithstanding, the use of *steady* in this sentence reinforces the aspectual function that has been described thus far. The mind, through metaphorical extension, is the agent of the active/passive thought processes. Moreover, in order to perform all of its vital duties, the mind must operate in a persistent fashion. The essential point is relatively simple: the human mind is a source of constant intensive activity, which is the quality that makes cognitive activity eligible for aspectual marking with *steady*.

One final anecdote is altogether different from anything we have considered until now. Some additional background information is therefore necessary. The majority of these data were initially collected while I was a lifeguard in Los Angeles and Philadelphia. This example is derived from the Los Angeles data. With the exception of one other fellow and myself, there were no other black lifeguards on the staff. The city, having experienced some racial tensions at other public pools, had hired some former convicts—all of whom were African American—as bouncers to protect the staff. A few of the local male teenagers considered it to be a great sport to sneak into the girls' dressing room. The bouncers would then retrieve them. Later, the males would sneak in again, and the cycle continued on a regular basis. The pool was a local gathering spot, and the older teens congregated near the entrance, although they seldom purchased a ticket to swim. On the day in question one of the male teens repeatedly ran into the girls' dressing room. His actions were especially annoying to the only bouncer on duty, because the bouncer's girlfriend had come by the pool to reconcile a disagreement. The couple would be engaged in hushed conversation, only to be interrupted by the cat-and-mouse antics of the teen who kept dashing into the facility. In exasperation the bouncer snapped, "Man, you just steady on everybody's case."

At first blush this example appears to be quite different, but as we shall see, the functional role of *steady* is unchanged. In spite of the different sentence structure, *steady* indicates that the actions of the teenager are intense, consistent, and continuous. The exceptional nature of this example is due to the idiomatic status of being on someone's case. Without going into great detail here, the prepositional phrase *on everybody's case* is perceived as an active process. In this regard the idiom functions very much like a progressive verb, and it is this progressive interpretation that allows *steady* to be applied in this case.

Other prepositional phrases—more specifically, those that are not associated with habitual or durative events—are unacceptable with *steady*. For example, AAVE speakers categorically rejected sentences like '*The baby is steady under the table' or '*They be steady on the couch.' Only those prepositional phrases that are associated with active processes are potential candidates for AAVE *steady*.

These functional examples bring us to the next phase of the research, namely, the collection of additional data. It was clear that the tape-recorded corpus, which consisted of numerous hours of interviews, would be insufficient. And the other sentences that were transcribed by hand were quite capricious. Since most of the observed sentences were restricted to the present tense, several questions remained regarding the acceptability of *steady* with different tenses, as well as the syntactic position of the adverb itself. It was therefore necessary to design a questionnaire to test the parameters for *steady,* without drawing too much attention to the form itself.

DATA COLLECTION AND SYNCHRONIC INSIGHTS

A total of seventy-eight subjects completed the questionnaire. Forty are residents of Los Angeles, and the remaining thirty-eight live in Philadelphia. Each of the informants is an adult member of the AAVE community. As such they are mature speakers who have had prolonged exposure to the vernacular. And, to insure access to the most representative speakers, the results presented here (see Table 3) are limited to evaluations by active participants in the black vernacular culture.

This procedure insures that individuals like myself, who have had extensive exposure to SE, are not biasing the vernacular sample. The questionnaires were introduced in the fourth year of a larger long-term study of AAVE style shifting (Baugh, 1983, 1996). Because of this previous contact, all of the subjects had already provided lengthy linguistic interviews prior to my direct requests to complete the questionnaire.

As stated previously, the questionnaire was designed with several issues in mind. What influence does tense marking have on *steady*? Do different types of progressive verbs impact on acceptability judgments, or does adverb placement (i.e., the position of *steady* in the sentence) likewise

TABLE 3. Percentages of Acceptability in Response to the Questionnaire (see Figure 9); based on Distinctions in Tense for Progressive and Stative Verbs

Progressive Verbs

	Los Angeles				Philadelphia			
	1	2	3	4	1	2	3	4
sleeping								
present	73	18	9	0	68	26	6	0
future	63	24	13	0	62	35	2	1
past	85	15	0	0	82	16	2	0
working								
present	56	39	3	2	66	23	9	2
future	52	38	8	2	74	14	6	6
past	70	30	0	0	66	33	1	0
rapping								
present	90	5	3	2	84	15	1	0
future	79	15	4	2	74	14	8	4
past	98	2	0	0	89	11	0	0
running								
present	92	6	2	0	89	7	4	0
future	84	10	5	1	80	9	8	3
past	97	3	0	0	92	5	3	0

Stative Verbs (cf. Lakoff 1966)

	Los Angeles				Philadelphia			
	1	2	3	4	1	2	3	4
knowing the truth								
present	9	19	28	44	5	8	48	39
future	2	7	32	59	1	4	62	33
past	0	5	30	65	0	5	50	45
knowing everybody's business								
present	61	21	12	6	40	29	1	16
future	41	27	17	15	36	28	17	19
past	65	15	20	0	50	21	24	5
having money								
present	17	54	15	14	18	35	43	4
future	7	50	16	27	13	32	50	5
past	30	40	8	22	21	21	55	3
resembling his father								
present	0	6	12	82	1	0	11	88
future	0	0	6	94	0	0	8	92
past	3	3	12	82	0	2	13	85

N for Los Angeles = 40
N for Philadelphia = 38
Total *N* = 78

influence acceptability? These modifications are best illustrated by the general questionnaire format itself:

Questionnaire Format According to Tense and Adverb Placement

Present Tense

1. He steady Verb + ing.
2. He be steady Verb + ing.
3. He steady be Verb + ing.

Future Tense

4. He gon be steady Verb + ing.
5. He gon steady be Verb + ing.
6. He steady gon be Verb + ing.

Past Tense

7. He was steady Verb + ing.
8. *He steady was Verb + ing (not included on questionnaire).

Various verbs were substituted in the preceding format, with the exception of example 8, which is ungrammatical. The preliminary objective was to establish a statistically reliable quantitative analysis with respect to the preferred verbs, tenses, and adverb placement. The final results did not achieve this ambitious objective, although the preferred environments for *steady* have clearly been established (see Table 3).

It was necessary to record the questionnaires on tape. Two male AAVE speakers from Los Angeles provided this oral questionnaire; two critical problems were immediately resolved by this practice. Many of the best AAVE informants have not had adequate opportunities to master reading skills. Any direct request to have them read might therefore have triggered an embarrassing situation. An oral questionnaire also controls intonation as a constant variable. Had the subjects been presented with written questionnaires, it would have been very difficult to control the intonation patterns that they would impose on various sentences.

All subjects responded to questionnaires using the format presented above, that is, where various verbs, tenses, and adverb placements were substituted. In an effort to make this study seem more relevant to the informants, while at the same time drawing their attention away from direct scrutiny of different verbs, all subjects were asked to compare every *steady* sentence (which they heard on tape) with their own impression of whether or not the same sentence would be improved by substituting *always*. Each *steady* sentence was initially graded based on the following questionnaire scaling code:

1. Most Black people could say this naturally.
2. A lot of Black people could say this naturally, but some would not.
3. Some Black people might say this, but most would not.
4. Most Black people wouldn't say this at all.

Upon ranking each of the *steady* sentences, the subjects would then respond subjectively with their own sentence using *always*; in this instance *always* served as a contrast conception, drawing attention away from the different verbs, tenses, and adverb placement.

The most significant results from the questionnaire are presented in detail in Table 3, but the essence of the results can be stated simply. The boundary of acceptability between progressive and stative verbs was reconfirmed by the questionnaire, and the unique aspectual function of AAVE *steady* was revealed most clearly when various subjects began to volunteer opinions on their perceptions of critical linguistic distinctions with the past tense. When asked the difference between *steady* and *always,* one of the informants stated the case as follows:

> Yeah, like . . . see . . . let's say, like . . . you know, "he was steady rappin' " . . . uh . . . that don't mean he was always rappin. If he was always rappin', his rap might not be steady at all.

While the preceding comment may appear at first glance to be a tautology, the primary observation reinforces the functional differences between *always* and *steady.* Another comparison to SE sheds additional light on the issue; in SE and AAVE, 'She was always jumping' implies that her actions should be associated with several previous episodes ('every time I saw her she was jumping'). For AAVE speakers this contrasts with 'She was steady jumping' because this usually refers to the activity of a single past event. Some AAVE speakers could therefore say, 'She was always steady jumping' without being redundant. The fact that *steady* usually refers to a single activity, albeit habitual or durative, is another factor that helps to preserve its unique status in AAVE. Challenging questions still remain regarding *steady,* especially the historical ones, and I hope that readers of this book and others who are interested in AAVE will study this aspectual marker in greater detail. In the meantime I hope that educators and linguists may benefit from some of these preliminary observations of this camouflaged form.

10

Come Again

Discourse Functions in African American Vernacular English

Spears (1982, 850) describes *come* in African American vernacular English [AAVE] as expressing "only speaker indignation." *Come* has the capacity to convey other moods as well. Depending on pragmatic constraints within various discourse contexts, *come* may be fully camouflaged or partially camouflaged. This chapter identifies some of these alternative moods, along with the introduction of gradient degrees of camouflage. These observations complement Spears' (1982) original analysis and provide further support for the special status of camouflaged forms in linguistic inquiry.

    Come is also employed in Southern vernacular English [SVE]. Both dialects use *come* to convey personal observations or opinions. Although *come* occurs most frequently in narratives that discuss some past episode(s), it may also occur in the present or future tense.

STANDARD ANALYSES OF *COME*

Fillmore's (1966) analysis of the deictic implications for *come* in standard English, as well as Lakoff's (1974) complementary observations regarding *this* and *that,* reveal some well-known insights for this form. These analyses are relevant to the present study insofar as they pertain to the variable nature of camouflaged *come* in AAVE.

In some sentences, such as

1. We will come to the meeting.
- or -
2. He is coming home.

we see that standard English (SE), AAVE, and SVE share identical semantic interpretations. Such examples do not represent instances of camouflage, because speakers of different dialects use the verb in the same linguistic manner. Some other examples are not so clear:

3. Don't come (running) in here without wiping your feet!
- or -
4. We come (running) when we hear the fire alarm.

Examples 3 and 4 could be classified as instances of *partial camouflage;* speakers of AAVE, SE, and SVE could interpret these sentences differently, because some dialects use *come* as a semi-auxiliary (see Spears 1982, 851), while SE does not. As a result, we find that camouflaged forms may constitute an important source of (potential?) linguistic confusion. Thus, while AAVE and SVE share the same linguistic characteristics that have been observed by Fillmore (1966), Binnick (1971), and Clark (1974), these vernacular dialects also employ *come* in other grammatical roles.

This survey demonstrates that *come* in AAVE and SVE has significant semantic overlap with other semantic characteristics for *come,* which should be expected. The point that I seek to stress by this observation is that we can now identify three distinct divisions for *come*: (a) standard verbal usage, including idiomatic usage such as "He will come up with the right answer," (b) partially camouflaged *come,* as illustrated in statements 3 and 4 above, or (c) fully camouflaged *come,* which is discussed in more detail below.

UNIQUE PROPERTIES OF *COME* IN AAVE AND SVE

Limitations within the present corpus prevent full evaluation of the historical evolution and implications associated with the unique grammatical properties of *come* for AAVE and SVE. These diachronic issues are not trivial, and to the best of my knowledge, the historical association between

AAVE and SVE is still controversial among various scholars in the field. However, as Wolfram (1974) observed, one need not have a full picture of the relevant historical facts if the object of analysis is synchronic. As stated at the outset, this analysis seeks to provide evidence that complements Spears' (1982) previous investigation of this form in AAVE.

He observed *come* in sentences like the following:

5. He come walking in here like he owned the damn place.
6. He come trying to hit on me.
7. She come going in my room, didn't knock or nothing.
8. He come coming in here raising all kind of hell.

Spears also distinguishes between sentences that he observed in natural speech (primarily gathered at a beauty salon) and his own linguistic intuitions regarding this form. The implications for fieldwork in the AAVE community are discussed below. Nearly all of the naturally occurring sentences reflect *come* as an emphatic marker, often in the historical present. And, again, as Spears observes, most of his examples convey speaker indignation. However, upon closer examination we find that indignation is not a requisite mood for *come,* but one of many possible moods. For example, in a sentence like "He come telling me how fine I was," other moods could easily prevail under different pragmatic circumstances. As new data indicate, this identical remark could be stated with neutral-to-positive emotional reactions, especially if the statement is made by the object of the hearer's affection. In other words, if the woman liked the man who told her she was fine, her comment might not convey indignation, but some other more positive reaction. These different moods are often conveyed by variations in intonation; that is, in much the same way that intonation conveys anger or joy in other spoken discourse.

In addition to such positive reactions, the very same statement could be used to convey hope, skepticism, and even combinations of these reactions. The nature of the variability is complex, but this linguistic elasticity, regarding mood, tense, and aspect, allows AAVE and SVE speakers to convey a broad range of moods, albeit conveyed through nontraditional usage. Thus, staying with the same example, alternative pragmatic and discourse contexts could refer to a full spectrum of emotions, including:

- outright indignation
- indignation combined with disbelief
- disbelief

- disbelief combined with hope
- hope combined with belief
- hope, as the foremost response

This continuum is illustrative, and not intended to delimit the full range of possible combinations of moods that can be conveyed with AAVE and SVE *come.*

DATA COLLECTION

Due to the grammatical complexity of AAVE *come,* Spears devotes primary attention to linguistic details in favor of the rudimentary aspects of fieldwork in the AAVE community. He claims that the highly emotive status of *come* delimits the value of traditional tape recorded interviews. Like Wolfson (1976), Spears assumes that interviews will automatically have an inhibitory effect on speech behavior. Elsewhere (Baugh 1980, 1983) I argue that socio-linguistic interviews need not stifle ordinary discourse, that is when field-worker's show ethnographic sensitivity toward their informants. Despite personal familiarity with *come,* I am reluctant to rely exclusively on my own linguistic intuitions regarding this form. The present analysis is therefore derived from fully representative members of AAVE and SVE communities.[1]

I have been fortunate, because I have had many positive experiences with my fieldwork in the black community. It has been my experience that there is a deep and abiding interest in black culture in the AAVE commu-nity, which should come as no surprise. All communities share ethnocen-tric curiosity, seeking to know as much as they can about their own group and what they share with others who have (dis)similar backgrounds.

I was able to introduce this topic to AAVE and SVE informants in Texas, and AAVE informants in California. The data are derived from three primary sources: interviews, recorded narratives, and completed question-naires. These new data confirm Spears' original observation that the vast majority of "*come* # Vb + ing" sentences convey speaker indignation to-ward some past event. Moreover, an elementary transformation [(come # Vb + ing)—> Vb + ed] will produce an SE equivalent, albeit with less emphasis than AAVE/SVE usage with *come.*

In order to evaluate the range of moods, tenses, and possible impli-cations for aspectual marking, questionnaires were developed based on Spears' (1982) original discussion, as well as other examples derived from my own fieldwork and that of Kathy Lewis, who served as the primary fieldworker in her native community of East Austin, Texas.[2]

The initial impetus for this study comes from Spears, because he was the first to introduce the concept of linguistic camouflage into comparative studies between AAVE and SE. I also found some similar examples within my Los Angeles corpus. The following excerpt appears to confirm Spears's observation that AAVE *come* is used to convey indignation.

I recorded this interview in 1974 while gathering data in Los Angeles from AAVE informants. The woman who is speaking is well known to me; we had worked for the City of Los Angeles in the Parks and Recreation Department for several years; I was interviewing her and we were discussing the topic of 'relationships.' It was largely coincidental that the topic had immediate relevance to her life; her husband had been cheating on her, and she had just confirmed this painful fact by finding him at another woman's home:

> So she called back and hung up, and then she called again and he answered. So she say "Where are you?" He didn't go to work that night. He went to where she was and stayed there all night and half the next day. And then he got the nerve to come telling me he was with this dude that owns a wig shop and I don't even know who he is.

Several other AAVE speakers—who listened to these interviews at my request—challenged the observation that her remark was indignant, based primarily on their impression of her intonation; these informants claimed that her emotion was more disbelief than anger; still others argued in favor of pure indignation or a combination of emotions. This lack of agreement, on the part of several AAVE speakers who heard the same remarks, led me to investigate *come* in more detail.

The first steps included preliminary reexamination of our AAVE data from Los Angeles, to determine the relative frequency of this usage in everyday discourse. This effort yielded several examples, including:

9. Don't come telling me all those lies.
10. She better not come tripping in here all high again.
11. He always come talking that same old bull.

The sentences with bare infinitives are very similar to comparable sentences in SE, although the emphatic intention of *come* in AAVE and SVE is overt, whereas "Don't (come) tell (+ ing) me how to do my job(!)" may or may not be stated in an emphatic (or perhaps indignant) manner.

These sentences, among others that were recorded from AAVE informants, provide the first evidence suggesting that we are dealing with variable degrees of camouflage. Since all of the relevant evidence from our interviews employed *come* in reported speech, we began to conduct new interviews in Austin, Texas, to test the correspondence between AAVE *come* and tense marking. In other words, we tried to determine if *come* would occur in all tenses, or was this usage limited to one or two tenses, but not others. Briefly, AAVE semi-auxiliary *come* can occur with all tenses, but there is a marked preference for historically present usage in ordinary discourse. This probably has a great deal to do with *come*'s role as an emphatic marker.

We therefore focused our new interviews on narratives, although we structured the interviews so that our questions were designed to elicit responses (i.e., narratives) referring to the past, present, and future of a particular topic or event; there are pragmatic restrictions with this procedure, because interviews can easily be perceived as highly contrived once fieldworkers begin to organize questions in a strict or highly formulated (i.e., nonspontaneous) manner. Thus, we intentionally manipulated the tense referent of our questions in an effort to fully evaluate the tense restrictions, if any, that are associated with AAVE *come*.

This procedure yielded further insights, including the possibility of alternative forms of linguistic camouflage. Spears (1982, 850) argues for a distinction between verbal *come,* for all speakers of English, and indignant *come* in AAVE. The new evidence suggests that we may not be dealing with a binary contrast, but a complex array of variable moods. Spears' view, which is highly plausible, limits camouflage to nonstandard usage. An alternative interpretation would call for the notion of camouflage to extend to the verbal form of *come* as well.

The theoretical distinctions between these interpretations are considerable, and I will only touch on the issue briefly. Spears' original discussion—calling for two distinct forms of *come*—relegates the parameters of camouflaged forms to their nontraditional uses (see Example 1). The expanded interpretation of camouflage would include both standard and nonstandard uses of the form in question, and then—by comparative means or other reliable procedures—would determine variable degrees of camouflage as they pertain to specific examples (see Example 2):

Example 1: Discrete camouflage
A. Shared uses = No camouflage
B. Unique nonstandard uses = Camouflaged forms

Example 2: Variable camouflage
A. Shared uses = Minimum camouflage
B. Partial semantic overlap = Partial linguistic camouflage
C. Unique nonstandard uses = Maximum linguistic camouflage (due to a
lack of shared linguistic characteristics)

In either view, the concept of linguistic camouflage is shrouded by
nature, and will remain a topic of considerable interest to linguists who
study language in use.

DESCRIPTION OF RESULTS

The procedures outlined above are limited in many respects, but they nevertheless provide us with sufficient evidence to make some significant observations, building upon Spears' (1982) initial discovery. Of considerable
importance, we now know that AAVE *come* has the capacity to convey a
broad range of moods, not merely indignation. Much less clear are the fluctuating interpretations of this form by various informants.

In order to control intonation as a constant (i.e., nonvariable) factor,
our questionnaires were recorded on tape by native AAVE speakers, including young male and female adults. This procedure also allowed us to gather
data from informants who have not had adequate opportunities to master
the basic literacy skills that would be needed to complete a written questionnaire. We used network techniques, similar to those adopted by Milroy
(1980), Bortoni (1985), and Poplack (1978). Once contacted, informants
were asked to listen to a series of short comments (including some brief
narratives) that employed *come*. They were then asked to identify the tense
and mood associated with the relevant *come* sentence; again, these sentences were presented in discourse contexts, thereby providing sufficient
pragmatic content so that informants were able to draw more reliable
conclusions.

In almost every case informants disagreed about the intended moods
associated with various statements. The dominant trend favored Spears' interpretation, with the added provision that some examples were stated in
the historical present. However, another anecdote reflects *come*'s linguistic
versatility in AAVE. Many of my interviews with young men include tall
tales and capricious combinations of truth, fiction, and local legends. The
interview in question derives from a young man who was telling me and a
few other men (all in our mid-twenties at that time) about a woman who
made a pass at him:

I was just, you know, standing by my ride [car] at the dam [a man-made lake] when she come walking up to me, put her hand on her hip, and go like this. [He then raised his arm, placed the other hand on his hip, and, with all of the feminine charm he could muster, he mimicked her [alleged] beckoning gestures with his extended index finger, and alluring facial expressions that were intended to suggest that 'come hither' look.]

The essential observation, once again, is that AAVE *come* conveys moods that exceed indignation. The truth of the preceding remarks were challenged by several of his peers, because some knew the young lady and did not believe she would do such a thing. Nevertheless, even if the speaker is lying, *his* use of *come* in this context is intended to express braggadocio or perhaps desire, but clearly he was not conveying indignation.

Despite the fact that the moods and tenses associated with *come* are highly variable, and that discourse context plays a considerable role in specific grammatical interpretations, the striking common denominator is that *come* is used to report about a previous event, or make some prediction about the present or future. This is also the case for SVE, particularly among working-class white Southerners, who share similar linguistic intuitions regarding nonstandard uses for *come*.[3]

For the sake of expedience it is most convenient to consider these preliminary findings in qualitative terms. Consider the following:

10. Don't mess with my old lady.
11. Don't be messing with my old lady.
12. Don't go messing with my old lady.
13. Don't come messing with my old lady.

Black and white informants were asked to evaluate these sentences with respect to similarities or differences in meaning. Most SE speakers made some clear distinctions. Example 10 tended to be preferred by SE speakers, in a generic sense, while example 11 had a progressive interpretation. Example 12 suggests that the 'old lady' is not at the speaker's location at the time of the utterance, and example 13 implies the opposite, namely, that the speaker is making the statement in the location where one would expect to find his 'old lady.'

Some AAVE and SVE speakers share many of these linguistic impressions, but not necessarily all of them. First, SVE speakers made the standard deictic distinctions for examples 12 and 13, but these appear to share the durative interpretation of example 11. What is most striking is that a majority of AAVE informants claimed that examples 12 and 13 were inter-changeable.

Despite the tentative and qualitative nature of these observations, there can be no doubt that speakers of different dialects of American English use *come* in alternative ways. One reason that these special grammatical properties have tended to go unnoticed is that they are concealed, or camouflaged, as Spears suggests. This notion of *camouflage* may be somewhat confusing, because the camouflage lies within the confines of a coincidental lexicon, not coincidental grammatical roles.

LIMITATIONS OF THE PRESENT STUDY

This examination has several limitations. As mentioned, important diachronic issues are inherent to this study; at this stage of analysis I have not had an adequate opportunity to fully evaluate the relevant historical data. I am therefore reluctant to engage in speculation regarding the temporal dimensions pertaining to semi-auxiliary *come*. Another limitation grows out of the corpus itself. As our analyses of nonstandard dialects becomes refined, our attention has shifted from the common (frequently occurring) distinctions between SE and AAVE. Rickford's (1975) examination of stressed *been* illustrates the point at hand.

At the time Rickford began his examination of stressed *been*, Labov believed that his New York AAVE corpus was devoid of such usage. However, because I was evaluating copula variability from that corpus at that time, I did discover a few examples of stressed *been* that had not been detected previously. Due to the specialized discourse role of stressed *been*, it did not appear in our corpora with the high levels of frequency that were common in the earlier studies of, say, negative concord, consonant cluster reduction across morpheme boundaries, and copula variation. Stressed *been* simply appeared less regularly in ordinary discourse than did other distinctive characteristics of AAVE. Spears (1982) and Baugh (1983) experienced similar methodological problems with their respective investigations of *come* and *steady* for AAVE (see Chapter 9); like stressed *been*, the highly specialized function of these camouflaged forms helped to conceal them from detailed linguistic scrutiny.

The incorporation of questionnaires and new interviews has been provided in an effort to overcome some of the limitations associated with our general interviews. Another limitation was also mentioned previously because AAVE scholars who happen to be black may feel free to call upon their own linguistic intuitions as a source of reliable data, while others, like myself, feel that extensive personal exposure to SE requires that we confirm our linguistic impressions with the most representative AAVE speakers (i.e., those who have not had extensive contact with SE beyond their colloquial community).

IMPLICATIONS FOR FUTURE RESEARCH

The preceding limitations also point to the areas where future research is needed. Of greatest importance, it will be useful to determine the etymology of AAVE and SVE *come*. These historical insights may in turn shed additional light on the synchronic variation that has been described herein.

The implications for data collection for AAVE or other languages among oppressed peoples remains to be seen. For example, Chomsky (1977) has argued that "from a linguistic point of view" the study of English is the same. However, based on my extensive contact in the AAVE community I know this is not the case. One cannot merely approach the AAVE informant on the street with a clipboard and solicit linguistic judgments in the same manner that graduate students in linguistics ponder grammatical parameters.

The obvious reason for this lies in society, not within the language itself. However, these social impressions are essential to our linguistic goals. As a young child I was taught that my native dialect was "bad English." Like so many other AAVE students in our public schools, I came to believe—as I was told by my teachers—that my native dialect was "ungrammatical." Thus, after years of being bombarded with the notion that "I ain't got none" is ungrammatical, few, if any, true AAVE speakers are capable of providing unbiased grammaticality judgments. It is therefore useless to use linguistic barometers of "well formedness" when native speakers of the object of linguistic inquiry have been taught that their well-formed sentences are ungrammatical.

I have not mentioned the educational implications of this research, in part, because of the tentative nature of these observations. Nevertheless, the role of linguistic camouflage for children in our public schools is considerable, because such camouflage provides critical instances where students can become confused, and do so without immediate detection on the part of educators. Since this potential for student confusion exists, linguists might well begin to compile examples of such forms and show how their usage varies across dialects. This type of information should be stored in a manner that would be readily available to teachers, along with helpful suggestions on how to use the evidence to the educational advantage of the student. While educational concerns may seem obvious, they often are taken for granted, and I do not wish to perpetuate that trend.

CONCLUSION

I have attempted to demonstrate that the AAVE *come* encompasses all tenses, several moods, and has aspectual versatility, thereby suggesting shades of 'gradient camouflage.' This notion of variable camouflage is important in cross-dialect studies, such as those between AAVE and SE, because there are occasions where speakers of the language—in this case, English—share semantic interpretations. This semantic overlap results in two definitions of linguistic camouflage: (1) unique nonstandard usage is associated with camouflage, while shared uses are not considered to be camouflaged, versus (2) variable degrees of camouflage, where shared uses are seen as being maximally camouflaged (i.e., they share many characteristics), and unique uses within various dialects of the language are minimally camouflaged (because they share few characteristics). As homophones, camouflaged forms are deceptive, and have been resistant to precise linguistic scrutiny.

The present survey seeks to expand our understanding of *come* in AAVE and thereby expand upon Spears' original formulation of linguistic camouflage. This enterprise may have positive social and educational consequences as we provide more thorough descriptions of these forms, because they represent a significant source of linguistic confusion among speakers of different dialects of English, and possibly speakers of other languages with comparable homophonic camouflage.

Hypocorrection

Mistakes in the Production of African American Vernacular English as a Second Dialect

African Americans who have learned standard English (SE) natively comprise a minority group within a minority group. Some of these individuals, in attempts to demonstrate solidarity with inner-city blacks, will shift style (i.e., accommodate) toward vernacular black speech. These efforts to accommodate occasionally exceed prevailing linguistic norms for African American vernacular English (AAVE), resulting in the creation of hypocorrect utterances, instances of linguistic overcompensation beyond the target linguistic form. The majority of such examples occur with camouflaged forms, which Spears (1982) defined as lexical items that serve different grammatical and semantic functions for the standard and nonstandard dialects of a language.

Throughout this chapter I refer to two similar terms: *hypercorrection* and *hypocorrection*. Hypercorrection is an older term, applied to instances where nonstandard speakers surpassed the standard. Hypocorrection derives its name from the social trajectory of linguistic change—from SE toward (and beyond) nonstandard AAVE.

DeCamp (1971) observed that hypercorrection is a distinct sociolinguistic phenomenon. Not only does one observe linguistic variation, but there is also linguistic overcompensation, as nonstandard speakers provide "too much" linguistic information in their attempts to produce standard English as a second dialect.

This paper considers what happens when black SE speakers attempt to produce nonstandard dialects. To answer this we must also consider the social circumstances that have fostered this linguistic trend. Solidarity among African Americans in the inner city is preserved, at least in part, through usage of nonstandard vernacular norms. Many blacks who have learned SE natively will strive to accommodate toward nonstandard speech in appropriate situations within the vernacular African American community. This discussion concentrates on hypocorrection: cases of linguistic overcompensation beyond a nonstandard linguistic target.

An idealized model of mutual second dialect acquisition in a bidialectal speech community is presented initially, to place the topic of hypocorrection in theoretical context and to illustrate the inherently social nature of hypocorrection. The controversy surrounding hypercorrection for black English is then reviewed, along with pragmatic suggestions calling for compromise between extreme interpretations. Hypocorrection is finally shown to reinforce observations regarding linguistic innovation among African Americans.

AN IDEALIZED MODEL OF MUTUAL SECOND DIALECT ACQUISITION

Consider, hypothetically, mutual second dialect acquisition in an idealized speech community. The members of this speech community share a single language that consists of two mutually intelligible, but distinctive, dialects. Moreover, there is a long-standing tradition among all members of this speech community of learning the other dialect as a sign, let us say, of respect. The speech community is homogeneous in every other way.

Figure 11 implies another idealized linguistic state: speakers of dialect A and dialect B are capable of mastering a second dialect, that is, when

FIGURE 11. Mutual second dialect acquisition.

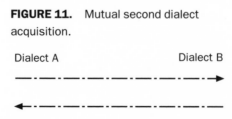

Dialect A   Dialect B

FIGURE 12. Mutual second-dialect acquisition
with linguistic variation.

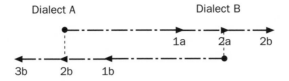

speakers of A produce B and vice versa, everyone does so without a trace
of their native accent.

Figure 12 illustrates a slightly different case, in which speakers of A
and B strive to master the second dialect but do so with varying degrees of
success (see Le Page and Tabouret-Keller, 1985): (1) undershooting the target
[i.e., 1a, 1b], (2) hitting the "other" linguistic target (producing nativelike
speech in the second dialect) [i.e., 2a, 2b], or (3) overshooting the target (i.e.,
hypercorrecting) [i.e., 3a, 3b]. Figure 12 is also an idealized model of mutual
second dialect acquisition, but it is more accurate than Figure 11 because it
accounts for differences in linguistic skill among speakers.

Since dialect A and dialect B have equal status in our hypothetical
speech community, we cannot attribute any of this linguistic difference to
social forces, and therein lies an obvious limitation of these models: typical
speech communities are composed of speakers who harbor strong linguistic
opinions. In the present hypothetical case, however, there are no social advantages or limitations associated with either dialect A or dialect B.

INHERENT SOCIAL PROPERTIES OF HYPOCORRECTION

Once social differences are added to Figures 11 and 12 our expectations
regarding linguistic change must account for the relative social value of each
dialect. Figure 13 illustrates a socially stratified speech community in which
a nonstandard dialect (spoken by members of the working class and the
poor) is devalued in comparison to a standard dialect, spoken by the middle
and upper classes, learned through formal education, and utilized by the
mass media.

MUTUAL SECOND DIALECT ACQUISITION IN A SOCIALLY
STRATIFIED BIDIALECTAL COMMUNITY

Hypercorrection is the result of linguistic redundancy created by efforts to
produce a second, institutionally valued, dialect. Hypercorrection always

FIGURE 13. A model of socially stratified hypercorrection and hypocorrection.

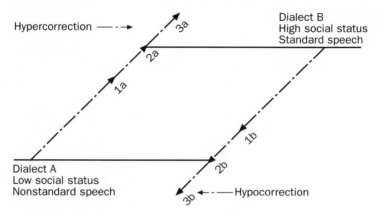

overshoots the intended standard target. Stated another way, hypercorrection always moves from the lower social classes toward the speech of elites, never the other way around. Hypocorrection introduces the less conceivable possibility that speakers of a standard dialect have made attempts to produce a nonstandard, second dialect, albeit with some linguistic overcompensation. It is not merely linguistic overcompensation, but overcompensation beyond the norms of a nonstandard dialect.

THE HYPERCORRECTION CONTROVERSY

Before turning to particular examples of hypocorrection we should first consider the hypercorrection controversy. After all, if hypercorrection is questionable, then certainly any concept drawn from it would also be suspect. Schneider (1982), Brewer (1986), and Pitts (1981, 1986) have called the concept of hypercorrection into question, specifically as it pertains to AAVE. Schneider and Brewer worked independently with data from Botkin's slave narratives and concluded that "hyper-s" had historical precedent in early English dialects, and that a specific durative function was being fulfilled by most hyper-s forms. On the basis of synchronic data, criticisms were raised by Pitts, who observed many instances of suffix-s that were "emphatic" rather than hypercorrect. He claims the suffix-s morphemes he observed were produced for conversational emphasis and were not the result of attempts to produce standard English as a target of linguistic aspiration.

The legitimacy of the concept of hypercorrection has little to do with the preceding debate regarding suffix-s variation in AAVE, because other examples of true hypercorrection can be found with this form and elsewhere in the grammar. Suffix-s has several functions, and some occurrences of suffix-s are hypercorrect, while others are emphatic; pragmatic considerations come into play when determining the actual grammatical function.

A fifty-eight-year-old woman from Shreveport, Louisiana, was being interviewed in a multiracial context with white classroom teachers, and in that situation—which was quite formal for this speaker—she said,

1. "I don't want no IQ teses for these childrens"
/aydonwʌn:oaykyutɛsɪzfoðiztʃIlənz/

where one could attribute her redundant usage of /-s/ to an attempt to speak "more properly" (i.e., traditional hypercorrection). Under different social circumstances, at a bowling alley in the vernacular AAVE community, a thirty-seven-year-old man bragged—to anyone who would listen—that he was the best bowler in the house, and he challenged anyone to match his boast. In the context of these remarks, he exclaimed,

2. "You know I wants to win!"
/yunoaywəntstəwIn/

The discourse context suggests that he was not emulating standard English; he used the emphatic /-s/ that Pitts (1981) describes.

Beyond /-s/ we find several cases of redundant past-tense marking, such as:

3. "He pickeded it up."
/hipɪktɪdɪdəp/
4. "They done lickeded the bowls and the spoons."
/ðeydənlIktIdððbowlzænððspunz/

As with the preceding examples, the burden of proof regarding hypercorrection, as opposed to some other form of morphological redundancy, stems from its directionality (from lower status to higher status dialects) and the linguistic overcompensation that results from attempts to produce standard English as a second dialect. Speaker intention is therefore vital to the final identification of hypercorrect forms; they occur when speakers strive to produce the standard. Other cases of redundant morphology are not hypercorrect.

BEYOND INFLECTIONAL MORPHOLOGY

The present operational hypothesis claims that hypocorrection is the social opposite of hypercorrection, but since most examples of hypocorrection have been morphophonemic, what are we to do with other linguistic evidence, evidence that is not morphological in nature but still demonstrates an overshoot of an intended linguistic target? Syntactic and phonological hypocorrection also occur.

Data from racially segregated interviews combined aspects of Giles and Powesland's (1975) accommodation theory with Labov's (1972b) contextual styles. It was necessary for speakers to provide informal conversation, but that conversation also had to reflect standard and nonstandard variability. Native AAVE and SE interviewers were employed in the hope that their interlocutors (i.e., the informants) would feel free to accommodate toward the fieldworker's dialect. This procedure produced some unexpected results. Two examples illustrate the need for a broader definition of hypocorrection.

EVIDENCE OF PHONOLOGICAL HYPOCORRECTION

Several examples of hypocorrection were found in the following linguistic environment:

$$[\Theta] \rightarrow <v>/[+vocalic] \_\_\_\_ \#.$$

A similar rule exists for AAVE:

$$[\Theta] \rightarrow <f>/[+vocalic] \_\_\_\_ \#.$$

Table 4 illustrates the range of variation associated with Figure 13 (1b, 2b, 3b).

All examples under 2b are common to AAVE, but the examples in 3b add the feature [+ voice], which exceeds AAVE. There are logical phonetic explanations for this process; since the vowel must be voiced, the hypocorrect forms maintain voicing throughout the word, while AAVE (2b) and SE (2a) employ voiceless consonants after vowels in the representative environment.

Another potential influence grows from the standard distinction be-

TABLE 4. Examples of Phonological Hypocorrection

Lexical example	1b	2b	3b
With	/∅/	/wɪf/, /wɪd/	/wɪv/
Both	/∅/	/bof/	/bov/
Tooth	/∅/	/tuf/	/tuv/
Booths	/∅/	/bufs/	/buvz/

tween singular /-f/ and ambiguous pluralization with /v + z/ as in "leaf/ leaves, knife/knives, life/lives," etc. Hypocorrect usage of /v/ may be reinforced by the existence of the phonological and phonemic contrasts found between /-f/ and /-v + z/ elsewhere in English phonology.

SYNTACTIC HYPOCORRECTION

Other interviews conducted by black fieldworkers provided examples of syntactic hypocorrection. These include sentences that were produced by black SE speakers during conversational interviews where they were accommodating toward AAVE.

Black fieldworkers were encouraged to employ vernacular norms, including slang, in an effort to provide conversational contexts where AAVE would be appropriate, regardless of the background of the informant. Many of the well-documented grammatical forms of AAVE were actively used by black interviewers, such as:

1. aspectual marking with *steady* (Baugh, 1984);
2. stressed *been,* used to mark distant past events (Rickford, 1975);
3. habitual and durative *be* (Fasold, 1972); Montgomery and Bailey, 1987);
4. semi-auxiliary *come* (Spears, 1982); and
5. multiple negation (Labov, 1972a) beyond isolated lexical variation, as a marked increase in the use of "man" by black SE males who were being interviewed by black males, e.g., "Yeah man," "Oh man!" "My man!" etc.

We find examples that employ novel syntax. One such example was produced during an interview between two black men. One was learning AAVE as a second dialect, and the fieldworker was a native speaker of AAVE. As the informant began to relax he offered more personal opinions, and on one occasion made some derogatory comments about his current, part-time, employer:

6. "He *steadily bes* on my case!" This combined use of *steadily* with *bes* is unattested in previous AAVE studies and suggests that the speaker is mixing AAVE *be(s)* with SE *steadily*. AAVE speakers would more readily produce the following sentences:

7. a. He be(s) on my case.
   b. He steady on my case (Inherent phonological neutralization.)
   c. He be steady on my case. (Inherent phonological neutralization.)
   d. He steady be on my case. (Inherent phonological neutralization.)
   e. He be on my case steady. (With heavy stress on final *steady*.)
   f. He(s) on my case steady. (With heavy stress on final *steady*.)

Although *steady* is a predicate adverb in AAVE (see chapter 9), it is not semantically or grammatically equivalent to SE *steadily*. In this case the SE speaker has produced something akin to traditional hypercorrection, in the sense that additional morphemes are added in the attempt to produce AAVE as a second dialect.

Another example is

8. "They *dones* blew them brothers away."

The informant, a black man from a predominantly white neighborhood near Dallas, was being interviewed by an AAVE fieldworker. In retelling the description of a gang war, he produced the preceding statement. AAVE does not employ suffix-s with perfective *done*. Since contact was maintained, the interviewer was able to ask follow-up questions of this informant. After listening to his interview he claimed that he was trying to emphasize the point and that /-s/ was making *done* "stronger."

SOME TENTATIVE IMPLICATIONS FOR CAMOUFLAGE THEORY

Spears' (1982) study of *come* in AAVE introduced the concept of camouflaged forms to black English research. Most of the hypocorrect examples occur with camouflaged forms; that is, AAVE and SE share many of the same lexical, morphological, and phonological properties, but there are instances where each dialect uses common elements for different grammatical purposes. Examples 6 and 7 are indicative of camouflaged forms.

Since most of the hypocorrect forms are camouflaged, in the sense that they exist in SE with different grammatical or semantic functions, we posit that second-dialect learners have experienced varying degrees of linguistic interference. In some cases they achieve their linguistic objective and successfully reproduce nonstandard norms, but during this process a combination of phonological, morphological, and syntactic features (occasionally) overshoot their intended target, and these examples are legitimate cases of hypocorrection.

AAVE AND COVERT PRESTIGE

Trudgill (1983) has studied the concept of covert prestige at length, and readers who are unfamiliar with this topic are encouraged to consult his work directly for a thorough account of this subject. Hypocorrection is also a by-product of the (c)overt linguistic prestige of AAVE, depending upon the circumstances, where nonstandard linguistic norms are deemed most appropriate. The covert dimension of this prestige grows from long-standing public devaluation of AAVE as "bad English," but tacit prestige prevails owing to the popularity of jazz and other African American verbal art forms.

Elsewhere (Baugh 1983) I discuss the educational and linguistic paradox that confronts most African American students. They are often expected to perform in two rather distinctive cultural contexts: the majority cultural context reinforces the overt value of SE; the street culture reinforces AAVE and provides an environment where dialect loyalty and in-group linguistic prestige can thrive. With the high visibility of African American music and visual arts, many people who have limited personal contact with AAVE speakers have, nevertheless, been exposed to many aspects of vernacular African American culture through mass media. Some of these portrayals are more accurate than others, but all serve to reinforce the factors that support (c)overt linguistic prestige. Educators continue to face these competing linguistic norms in their classes, and this trend is likely to prevail because of undaunted stereotypes that equate AAVE with low intelligence (Labov, 1972a; Farrell, 1983; Orr, 1987; Baugh, 1988).

CULTURAL IDENTITY THROUGH
SOCIOLINGUISTIC ACCOMMODATION

An undeniable dimension of hypocorrection is the direct result of linguistic accommodation to convey cultural allegiance to speakers of the target dialect. Le Page and Tabouret-Keller (1985) observed many instances where cultural loyalties were affirmed through the emphatic use and preservation of colloquial linguistic norms. Their research complements accommodation theory (Giles and Powesland, 1975) in the sense that black SE speakers have been observed to adjust their speech to perpetuate and preserve vernacular AAVE norms. Evidence for hypocorrection also reinforces the notion that "linguistic prestige" is conditioned by the social context of any given speech event.

Linguists are keenly aware of such matters, recognizing the substantive behavioral accommodations required, say, for an audience with royalty or the pope, as opposed to more casual conversations.

Speakers of standard dialects usually notice when hypercorrection occurs because of the striking difference from prescribed linguistic norms, and those who perpetrate hypocorrection tend not to be aware of their "mistakes." Popular stereotypes imply that a "nonstandard error" must be an oxymoron, but the following examples refute that interpretation. Each illustration was produced by a native speaker of standard English who attempted to replicate African American vernacular English:

9. Scott *bes* cute (said by a white female to a black female);

10. We *bes* the baddest frat (said by a white male to other white males);

11. They *been* (unstress) closed (said by a white male to a black female);

12. They *comes* talkin shit (said by a black male speaker of SE to a black male speaker of AAVE); and

13. He *comes* coming up to me all sweet, fixin to apologize (said by a white female to a black female).

In every instance, the standard speaker had no idea that (s)he had violated AAVE norms. Also, hypocorrection need not be produced by black SE speakers (see examples 9–11), nor need the recipient be black (as in example 10).

The popularity of rap music has also played a strategic role in the growth of hypocorrection, as more white speakers of the dominant dialect try to mimic stereotypical vernacular black speech. It is now common to find upper-middle-class youth gathered at suburban malls and resorts, publicly rehearsing their AAVE rap. Like anyone learning a second dialect, they tend to make mistakes on their road to partial fluency. Here I have attempted to identify some interesting instances of hypocorrection in everyday language, drawing upon diverse theoretical foundations in sociolinguistics, ethnolinguistics, accommodation theory, the sociology of language, and conceptual foundations from speech acts that convey cultural identity (see Le Page and Tabouret-Keller, 1985).

LIMITATIONS AND IMPLICATIONS
FOR FUTURE RESEARCH

We have not considered other significant sources of linguistic overcompensation in this initial examination of hypocorrection. Slang and speech acts that employ curses are two prime candidates for future hypocorrection research. Many AAVE informants observed that SE speakers use profanity "all wrong." These sentiments were expressed by a twenty-seven-year-old welder who had a black supervisor who was "lame" (see Labov, 1972a).

> 14. JR: The brother be trying, but he just don't know how to relax. Every time he see us he always be cursing and carrying on, even around the women, and you know that ain't right.
> J: [Do] You mean he don't know how to cuss?
> JR: No, no . . . that ain't it. When he be saying motherfucker this, and motherfucker that, he just don't use the right tone, and a lot of times he disrespects the women. He'll just keep right on bad mouthin even when an old lady come by.

This sense that SE speakers do not know how to perform AAVE speech acts is worthy of in-depth evaluation but exceeds the scope of the current discussion.

The qualitative introduction of hypocorrection, in linguistic terms, lays the foundation for future quantitative research. Here we have established the existence of hypocorrection, and identified that it thrives at different levels within the grammar. The theoretical consequences of this expanded definition of hypocorrection are considerable, because morphological (i.e., semantic) constraints are not the only means of exceeding linguistic targets in a secondary dialect. The issue of voicing, for example, hinges greatly on matters of voice onset/offset timing, which is an anticipated direction for future study.

CONCLUSION

The "divergence hypothesis" dominated AAVE literature during the last half of the 1980s, and has proved to be highly controversial. Some scholars claimed that black and white vernaculars were diverging (Labov and Harris, 1986; Myhill and Harris, 1986; Bailey, 1987), while others were skeptical (Rickford, 1987) or critical (Vaughn-Cooke, 1987) of these results. Proponents of the divergence hypothesis conducted interviews with vernacular AAVE informants and claimed grammatical divergence from standard English based on nonstandard English competence. Despite being second dialect learners, hypocorrect speakers are reinforcing linguistic divergence. Recalling that hypocorrection exceeds vernacular AAVE norms, it is divergent (from SE) by its very nature; it not only moves away from SE but goes beyond AAVE in the process. Thus, despite their native competence with SE, the hypocorrect speakers may be viewed as complementing black and white dialect divergence because they too are using language in innovative ways that are exceedingly nonstandard.

African Americans are pulled between competing linguistic forces from majority and minority cultures. The legacy of racial segregation has fostered this diversity. Although more blacks than ever have achieved positions of social prominence, far too many still suffer the consequences of poverty, and it is within this dynamic social context that hypocorrection exists. As far as the divergence hypothesis is concerned, hypocorrection reinforces observations made by proponents and detractors of the divergence hypothesis. The advocates are reinforced by hypocorrection because it diverges from SE at several points in the grammar. The fact that this process is taking place among blacks who already speak SE reinforces the social complexity among African Americans that Vaughn-Cooke (1987) raised when she criticized the divergence hypothesis. Hypocorrection reinforces that diversity and affirms the breadth of cultural and linguistic norms that coexist in African America. My remarks are offered in the hope that we may also broaden interpretations of linguistics prestige, as well as our appreciation for the intricate web of social and linguistic factors that influence language variation and change (see Labov 1994).

Linguistic Perceptions in Black and White

Racial Identification Based on Speech

This chapter evaluates reactions from 350 judges who were asked to record their impressions of different American English accents. In this instance the judges listened to eighteen individuals, including nine black and nine white speakers of American English. Readers who are familiar with Tucker and Lambert's (1972) pioneering research on attitudes toward black English will immediately recognize the extensive influence of their work here. However, the research at hand has a slightly different focus, drawing on aspects of Labov's (1972a,b, 1994) quantitative methods along with complementary insights from Rosch's (1973) work on perceptions, cognition, and the designation of semantic domains. Pinker (1994) has reviewed the development of human language in cognitive terms that are sensitive to matters of cultural diversity, which give rise to the variations in language that are of primary interest in this specific study.

In spite of the substantial literature on perceptions, relatively few sociolinguists have been actively involved with research on this topic. There are, of course, some noteworthy exceptions: Giles (1979), Brown and Levinson (1978), Heath (1983), and Fishman (1972a) are just a few of the scholars who have raised questions regarding the linguistic cues that define ethnicity and social borders—insofar as they can be determined through speech. All of us have experienced conversations with others who speak in a different accent, and we can usually specify whether our interlocutor's accent is ethnic, regional, and/or foreign. In spite of this ability for auditory discrimination, few of us can identify all of the particular linguistic cues and nuances that influence our capacity to detect dialect differences.

The long-range research goals are to specify the linguistic properties that are critical to auditory perceptions in general. By comparison, the immediate research objective is fairly simple; we hope to determine the relative sensitivity of different judges to differences between African American vernacular English (AAVE) and standard English (SE) accents. Before turning to specific details, however, a personal anecdote places this work in its proper social context.

A few years ago I took an extended sabbatical and moved temporarily to Stanford, to the Center for Advanced Study in the Behavioral Sciences. It was initially my intention to commute between San Francisco and Los Angeles on weekends to visit my wife and children, who were living with my parents. Thanks to support from directors of the center I was able to bring my family to Palo Alto, and toward this end I began making calls to locate a larger apartment.

Like some African Americans described by Taylor (1971), I am adept at style shifting, and during phone calls to inquire about apartments I adopted a semiformal manner of speech. It was never my intention to conceal my race; I had hoped to sound like a professional—which, after all, I am. So I made several appointments to visit prospective apartments. In two instances, upon my arrival I was told that none were available. In each case I informed apartment managers that I had phoned earlier to make an appointment. One manager denied that any appointment had been made, while the other indicated that there must have been some confusion. Regardless of their excuses, I was denied the opportunity to rent either of those apartments, and I strongly suspected this was due to my race. Since I used standard English during the phone calls, I questioned whether housing discrimination might be occurring during telephone conversations to members of ethnic or racial minority groups who could be identified as such by their speech alone. In other words, had I "sounded black" I probably would have been denied an appointment from the outset.

THEORETICAL FOUNDATIONS

Having introduced the personal motivation for this study, it is important to determine the extent to which speech can—and often does—serve as a social barrier and a (potential) badge of group identity. We must now turn to the question of how (and why?) listeners judge different accents in the ways that they do. As a black American linguist, I recognize that numerous social factors trigger stylistic variation in speech. Like most speakers anywhere, African Americans have the capacity to modify their dialect to meet the needs of different formal or informal speaking situations (Baugh 1983). It should therefore come as no surprise that some black speech is more readily identified with black people. On the other side of the coin, one need only look at any national news broadcast in the United States to know that some black Americans have completely mastered standard English. This diversity is somewhat similar to the range of dialects that can be found among other ethnic groups in America; some speakers preserve the ethnic vernacular, while others adopt standard speech patterns. Again, our goal here is to examine the relative sensitivity of hundreds of judges to different black and white dialects.

With this additional background in mind, we can now review the major research trends that form the theoretical foundations of this investigation. Since some of the current concepts grew out of visual perception studies, it is helpful to draw an analogy. Anyone who has studied elementary philosophy has pondered the question of color perception. Does one person view red or blue in the same manner as others do? Or is color perception just a reflection of cultural conformity? Here we ask the auditory equivalent: Do people hear the same speech in the same manner as do others who share the same language (but not necessarily the same dialect)?

In much the same way that Tucker and Lambert (1972) completed surveys on college campuses, I too have taken advantage of my ready access to students. However, I have also been careful to survey many consultants in the general public. Unlike Tucker and Lambert, I did not ask judges to evaluate several social characteristics; they were asked to place each speaker at a point on a linguistic continuum and provide their impressions of race or ethnicity. The present findings are therefore intended to complement the attitudinal studies developed by Tucker and Lambert (1972), Hoover (1978), and Fishman (1972a).

A main reason that direct references to social characteristics have been minimized in this study has to do with the strong attitudes held by so many

FIGURE 14. Perceptual comparison between auditory and visual systems.

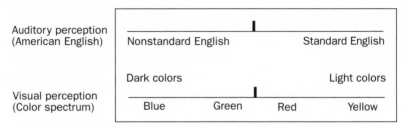

of the judges, be their opinions positive or negative. This fact is reinforced by the available literature on black and white language attitudes in the United States. There is a major limitation in the present approach, however, because judges did not consistently report their racial or ethnic perceptions. In other words, the judges evaluated every speaker, but not all judges specified their impression of each speaker's race (see Table 5). The relative assessment of racial perception is therefore tentative.

As mentioned, it would be futile to review the entire body of literature on perceptions. An excellent survey of early work on the subject is found in Emmett and Machamer (1976). The majority of experimental research has been psychological in orientation and largely concerned with cognition and the perception process. Phoneticians have also made great strides in auditory perceptual research (Abramson 1979). For sociolinguists and others it is important to appreciate that perceptions of linguistic differences are an integral part of the complete picture of language in society. Thus far we know that black and white speakers are sensitive to dialect differences, as displayed by the attitudes they hold (Kerr-Mattox 1987). Here we are concerned with a different orientation. Speakers are judged with respect to their relative position on a linguistic continuum, between standard English and (nonstandard) AAVE. The variables in this research are comprised of these fluctuating impressions.

Analytic procedures have been influenced to a significant degree by Labov (1972a, 1994) and Rosch (1973). For many years Labov has studied the variable nature of linguistic production. Here we incorporate aspects of his quantitative methods—within a variable paradigm—to study patterns of linguistic perceptions. Rosch has analyzed the varied reactions to the visual categorization of colors, providing vital insights as to how semantics and perceptions reinforce one another. The theoretical analogy is best illustrated in Figure 14, where visual perceptions of color are compared with auditory perceptions of different English accents.

PROCEDURES

Speech Selection

Speech stimuli were selected from a large corpus of AAVE speakers, including interviews where SE speakers participated (Baugh 1983). Also, some of the interviews were conducted in multiracial contexts, and three of the white speakers were selected from these. The other white speakers are educated Southerners, including male and female Texans and Georgians. Because the interviews cover a wide range of social topics, the content of each conversation was carefully screened to exclude discussions that were racial or ethnic in nature. For the most part the conversations dealt with such everyday topics as sports, cooking, or some local community issue that could have happened anywhere. Each speaker talked for 30 to 45 seconds, which is a considerable length of time for making perceptual evaluations of racial and/or ethnic identification.

The speech samples were first heard by linguists in an effort to establish an informal consensus with respect to the existence of a range of accents. Once suitable topics of adequate length were selected, they were randomly spliced onto two separate recordings. The two test recordings were used to reduce the possibility that the order in which the speakers were heard would influence their relative placement on the linguistic continuum. As suggested by the diversity of the speakers' social backgrounds, their speech reflects a wide range of dialects.

The Linguistic Sensitivity Test

Tucker and Lambert (1972) observe: "To be most useful, the rating scales provided listeners for evaluating speakers should be developed specifically for the samples of subjects to be examined [*sic*]" (1972, 176). The rating scale in this instance is rather simple. Judges were asked to listen to the recordings and place each speaker at a point along a linguistic continuum between standard and nonstandard English, based on their subjective impression of the speaker's linguistic background. One reason this floating scale has been introduced here is to determine the relationship—if any— between the social backgrounds of listeners and their relative sensitivity to, and evaluation of, various dialects. The linguistic sensitivity test has been developed in this way to restrict overt references to race, ethnicity, region, or social class (see Figure 15).

Regardless of the social setting in which the tests were given, the procedures were the same. All judges were told that they would complete a linguistic sensitivity test to determine their ability to place speakers on a

FIGURE 15.   Linguistic sensitivity test

Nonstandard English   Standard English

INSTRUCTIONS:

You are about to hear 18 different speakers. Each person will be discussing a variety of personal topics. The tape recording includes speakers from different regional and social backgrounds. In some instances the speakers have been influenced by strong nonstandard speech patterns; others speak what is commonly called 'standard English.' After you listen to each speaker, please identify your impression of his or her dominant linguistic background by placing that speaker's number at a corresponding position on the continuum; each speaker will be indentified by a sequential number.

There are no 'right' or 'wrong' answers to this test; the main objective will be to determine differences in linguistic sensitivity. The demographic information that is requested below will be very useful to the final results. Thank you for your help.

PLEASE COMPLETE THE FOLLOWING:

Age: _____ Place of birth: _____ Occupation: _____

Sex: _____ Present residence: _____ Education: _____
                       (City and/or county)
Native (1st) language: _____

Languages spoken other than English: _____

Languages spoken most frequently by you: _____

Your race or ethnicity: _____

Date:_____Location of test: _____

linguistic continuum, according to their (the judges') subjective opinion (see Figure 16). The initial phase of the test focused specifically and exclusively on the placement of speakers on an impressionistic linguistic continuum, and they were placed relative to the other speakers on the test recording.

Once the forms were distributed to the judges, one of the recordings was selected and played without interruption. In this way judges were initially given a sense of the full range of styles. It was only when they listened to the recording for a second and third time that they began to document their ethnic and racial impressions. Each judge was asked to identify the speakers in numerical sequence, by placing the number of the speaker onto a corresponding position on the continuum. The speakers were then heard again, twice in succession, so that the judges could concentrate on their evaluation. Table 5 illustrates the initial type of result, where variation exists within the quantitative pattern of the evaluations, and each speaker is represented by a range of reactions that span various portions of the continuum.

After judges completed this task they were asked to provide demographic information about themselves (see Figure 15) and they were asked to specify their impressions of the race or ethnicity of each speaker. As indicated previously, some judges did not complete this part of the procedure, and I suspect this was due to several factors, including strong personal convictions on the part of some judges—that is, they wished to avoid any calculus that might equate speech with racial or ethnic background. In any event, many of the evaluations do identify the racial or ethnic impressions of judges and, although the evidence is not complete, it is nevertheless of

TABLE 5.   Racial Identification of Eighteen Speakers Based on Speech

Subject	Number of responses	Race	% Identified as Black	% Identified as White
1	266	W	06	94
2	261	B	96	04
3	286	B	02	98
4	282	B	11	89
5	261	B	93	07
6	277	W	42	58
7	288	W	09	91
8	282	B	14	86
9	260	B	78	22
10	271	W	39	61
11	277	B	32	68
12	252	W	96	04
13	264	W	28	72
14	263	B	71	29
15	279	B	12	88
16	267	W	62	38
17	271	W	19	81
18	265	W	46	54

FIGURE 16.   Illustrations of variable linguistic evaluations by six judges.

Judge 1	5		2	4		1		3
			4					
Judge 2	5		2			1		3
Judge 3		5	2		4		1		3
Judge 4	5		2	4		1	3	
Judge 5		5		2	4		1	3
Judge 6		5	2		4	1	3	

Nonstandard English   Standard English

considerable interest. Most of the judges gave their impressions regarding the race or ethnicity of the speakers, presented in Table 5.

Data Specification

These procedures produced related databases, which laid the foundation for promising future research on dialect perceptions. The first and most revealing body of data consists of the cumulative reactions of the judges and the exposition of the range on the continuum that is attributed to each speaker. Because we already have extensive demographic information for the speakers, we can also draw tentative social correlations in relation to the judges' evaluations. I stress the tentative nature of these correlations due to the limited number of speakers on the test recording.

RESULTS

Possible Interpretations

There are two extreme possibilities with respect to these evaluations; namely, the judges may agree categorically, or they may completely disagree, placing each speaker at a different point on the continuum. Figure 17 illustrates this for hypothetical judges J_1-J_n. Figure 17a reflects 100 percent agreement and Figure 17b illustrates an instance where no judges agree. The actual results fall within these extremes and are illustrated in Figure 18 for all eighteen speakers. The evaluations illustrated in Figure 18 are restricted to judges who are native speakers of English. These results have also been adjusted to combine evidence from both test recordings;

speakers appearing in Figure 18 were presented in different sequences that are inconsistent with their numerical representation in Table 5.

As far as racial impressions are concerned, speakers 2, 5, 9, 12, and 14 were consistently identified as black Americans, although there are varying degrees of disagreement with respect to the linguistic purity of their AAVE. Be that as it may, these speakers used some slang expressions, along with nonstandard syntax and/or lexicon (e.g., "What it is?" or "They be gettin down at the park"). Other speakers, who were also identified as black Americans, did not use nonstandard syntax or slang, but their phonological pattern was clearly influenced by nonstandard norms (see Taylor 1971). At the other end of the spectrum, speakers 1, 3, 4, 7, 8, and 15 were always identified as white Americans, yet speakers 3, 4, 8, and 15 are black. The most interesting cases are those where no clear agreement can be found. Percentages for the available racial assessments are presented in Table 5.

Some judges were divided with respect to their opinion on the race or ethnicity of certain speakers. The reason this finding is noteworthy is that it reveals social relativity at work; judges have different degrees of linguistic sensitivity.

This brings us to some affiliated observations, more specifically to the correspondence between the judges' social backgrounds and their tendency to place speakers at different locations on the continuum. It is largely because a majority of the foreign judges evaluated speakers so differently that

FIGURE 17. Categorical perceptions of American English for eight hypothetical judges: *a,* categorical agreement by judges for one speaker; *b,* categorical disagreement by judges for one speaker.

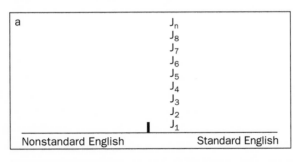

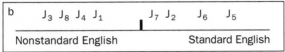

FIGURE 18. Variable dialect perceptions including race: *a*, of speakers who are regularly judged to be black; *b*, of speakers who are regularly judged to be white.

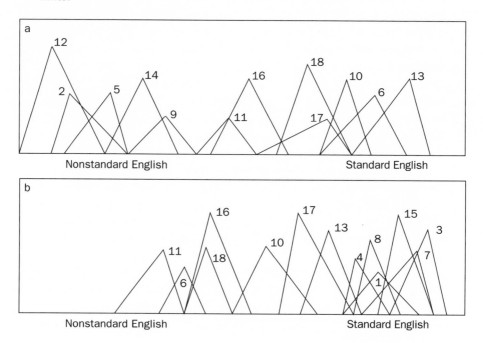

their collective impressions are not included in Figure 18. Although the 43 judges who learned English as a second language were able to make discriminations with respect to standard versus nonstandard speech, they tended to do so with greater polarity.

Native Evaluations and Second-Language Evaluations

The sharpest contrast to emerge from the results lies in the area of evaluations by native English speakers compared with those who have learned English as a secondary language (ESL). To illustrate this, four speakers have been singled out for comparison in Figure 19, which illustrates the gap between native and foreign judgments. The native English judges tended to cluster these speakers near the center of the continuum, whereas the ESL judges tended to place speakers in two broad camps at opposite ends of the spectrum, demonstrating that they are sensitive to linguistic differences, but not in the same ways as native English speakers. This should not be surprising, especially given the dominant social role of English in the United States.

There was also less agreement among ESL judges with respect to the ranked order of speakers; that is, regarding who spoke more or less (non)standard English. Some of the foreign judges remarked that they did not understand some of the speakers, and these were immediately placed at the nonstandard end of the continuum. There was also greater confusion on the part of the ESL judges with respect to racial identification; those at the nonstandard end were identified as black, although some of the Southern white speakers were occasionally identified as black by some of the ESL judges. The majority of those judged to be standard speakers were always identified as white. The white speakers were nevertheless identified as white standard speakers by other ESL judges, so there is no clear trend in this instance. Perhaps the most interesting difference between foreign and native racial assessments lies in the tendency for both groups to label the perceived standard speakers as white, yet four of these speakers are black.

FIGURE 19. Comparisons of four speakers by judges: *a*, who are native speakers of English; and *b*, who have learned English as a second language.

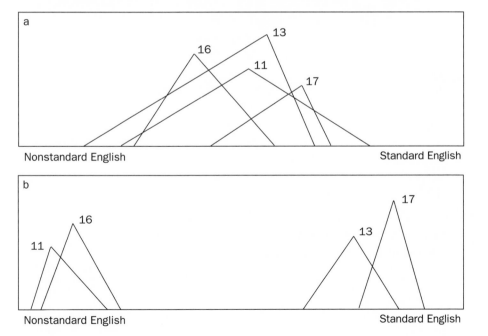

NATIVE JUDGES' EVALUATIONS BASED ON SOCIAL BACKGROUND

As indicated, native English speakers (N = 307) tended to rank the speakers in similar sequences but placed them at different points along the continuum. The relative positions were influenced more by the educational level of the judge than by other social characteristics, such as age, sex, race, or region. Educated judges were more likely to place speakers toward the nonstandard end, while less-educated judges were more likely to place speakers toward the standard pole of the continuum. This illustrates the type of social relativity that was mentioned before: those who have had extensive education seem to evaluate speech based on their experience, and they appear to be more critical in their judgment than those who have less education.

Some readers may be surprised to learn that racial background had very little influence on judges' decisions compared with their relative education. Less-educated whites generally placed more speakers at the standard end of the continuum than did college-educated blacks; the college-educated population was by far the most demanding in terms of identifying standard speakers, and this crossed racial, age, sex, and regional lines.

These preliminary results, which are limited, provide the foundation for ongoing experiments regarding various forms of linguistic discrimination. For example, Kerr-Mattox (1987) observed that many white teachers negatively judged African American students based on speech alone, and Tucker and Lambert (1972) were among the first to recognize that social discrimination against blacks is linked, at least in part, to pervasive negative stereotypes about black speech. Armed with the present results, and having suspected that I was once denied housing as a victim of racial discrimination, I have begun to test hypotheses that blacks (and Latinas/os) may be denied access to housing during telephone conversations, unlike my experience where such a denial was postponed until apartment managers were able to confirm my race during face-to-face meetings.

IMPLICATIONS FOR RESEARCH ON HOUSING DISCRIMINATION

Research is in progress that utilizes bidialectal and tridialectal speakers of American English to conduct a survey of housing discrimination through a series of controlled experiments that manipulate phonology, prosody and intonation, while syntax and semantics remain constant. AAVE, nonstandard Chicano English, and standard English are used by callers who always say, "Hello, I'm calling about the apartment (condominium, house) you have advertised in the paper." By controlling the linguistic stimuli in this way we eliminate grammatical or lexical variation, which often distinguishes one dialect from another, and concentrate exclusively on pronunciation differences.

We are compiling these results at the time of this writing, and it is too early in the investigation to confirm the hypothesis that speakers of nonstandard English, be it AAVE or Chicano English, are routinely "red-lined" (i.e., excluded) from consideration to rent or buy in areas where real estate agents and prospective landlords appear to show linguistic bias in favor of standard English. At this stage of analysis the results are regrettably predictable. Speakers of AAVE and Chicano English are routinely redirected to areas that are heavily populated by minorities, while standard English not only evokes a welcome reply in most cases, but also a reaction of surprise on the part of minority real estate agents and prospective landlords, who occasionally encourage standard English speakers to seek housing in predominantly white neighborhoods. Again, this discussion is preliminary, and the statistical evidence is forthcoming.

CONCLUSION

The analogy between visual perception and auditory perception has been applied to black and white speech in the United States through a series of experiments that began in the lab and moved toward social application in the continuing struggle for racial equality. As an African American linguist, I have had the ironic experience of converting my own distasteful experience with housing discrimination into a new vein of research which appears to confirm that the United States remains far from being the color-blind society that most Americans seek.

Although there is an obvious and intuitive linkage between racial background and linguistic behavior among many United States citizens, few scholars have explored the ways in which language is used as a means of perpetuating racial discrimination, and it remains my goal to use the tools of linguistic science to eliminate the barriers to social equality, justice, and opportunity that continue to be denied to many of our fellow citizens.

**PART
FIVE**

Conclusion

Research Trends for African American Vernacular English

Anthropology, Education, and Linguistics

ORIENTATION

In my view linguistic science is socially active. In much the same manner that physicists challenged European and Asian fascism during World War II, linguists can challenge racism, poverty, and uninformed linguistic chauvinism. This chapter is intended for readers who would like to know more about African American vernacular English (AAVE). The following survey is not comprehensive; it offers intellectual bridges for those who share my belief that linguists, and other concerned scholars, have an obligation to contribute to the equitable relief of citizens who are less fortunate (see Labov 1982; Rickford and Rickford 1995).

On December 18, 1997, the Oakland school board radically altered public perception of the linguistic legacy of American slavery when they voted unanimously to adopt a resolution declaring Ebonics the official language of the twenty-eight thousand African American students who attend school in that district. Most people, including linguists, were caught off guard by this Afrocentric classification that claimed to share no genetic affiliation with standard American English.

Readers of this work will probably recall Oakland's advocacy and eventual rejection of Ebonics (Baugh 1997, 1998; Nunberg 1997), but there have been numerous studies in various fields that focus squarely on the speech (and writing) of African Americans, and this chapter reviews some of those research trends.

We begin with a brief survey of technical linguistic analyses of AAVE, exposing some unresolved controversies. From there we explore educational applications and interpretations of linguistic findings, and those educational foundations take us back to the vernacular culture and community via anthropology. The chapter concludes with an appeal to scholars from different fields to lend their expertise to further clarification regarding the evolution of the complex consequences resulting from the African slave trade and to seek resolution of historical inequities that can withstand the political storms and controversy that now afflict affirmative action. American linguistic diversity provides an empirical foundation for a theory of sociolinguistic relativity that is inclusive of any person who uses language as a means of communication (either spoken or signed language), and does not rely on racial classification (see Figure 1 in Chapter 3, Figure 3 in Chapter 5, and Figure 20 later in this chapter). Readers will momentarily be encouraged to conduct a personal sociolinguistic diagnosis; for example, are you a native speaker of AAVE or not? Readers who are African American may come to this text with different linguistic impressions than might readers who are otherwise unfamiliar with African Americans or our culture. Without going into great detail now, we will soon combine Ogbu's (1978) castelike groups with the three linguistic divisions to create a heuristic linguistic diagnostic for the United States. These divisions in turn could easily be contrasted with social class status or other traditional sociological categories. Potential areas for future research are described within the context of closing remarks that call for greater scholarly engagement in the all-too-elusive quest for social equality.

A SURVEY OF TECHNICAL LINGUISTIC ANALYSES OF AAVE

When Bloomfield (1933) first spoke of AAVE, he did so from two perspectives; he confirmed that some viewed it as "bad" or "vulgar," although linguists preferred the more neutral term "nonstandard English." Many people still share misguided perceptions of AAVE, especially in the wake of the Ebonics controversy (Chapter 1, Baugh 1997). Labov (1972a), Shuy (1964), Wolfram (1969), Fasold (1972), and Stewart (1967) were among the first linguists to analyze AAVE as a coherent linguistic system worthy of scholarly attention. Standard English (SE) differs from AAVE, but it is not in any way superior in purely linguistic terms. During the 1960s it was common to find references to nonstandard Negro English (NNE), accompanied by debates about controversial historical interpretations of contemporary black speech. Dillard's (1972) *Black English* captured broad public attention, as scholars, educators, and general readers came to better understand linguistic vernaculars that were born of slavery. *Language in the Inner City* by Labov (1972a) was not historically oriented and focused instead on technical linguistic analyses and related educational issues. Dillard's work, having been strongly influenced by the creolist hypotheses espoused by Stewart, bolstered aspiring black pride and nationalism, based largely on the case that black English retained many Africanisms that survived the Atlantic crossing. In an effort to integrate studies of AAVE within Chomsky's emerging research paradigm, Labov (1969a) modified the formal linguistic rule notation first developed by Chomsky and Halle (1968).

Labov's efforts to bring AAVE studies into the linguistic mainstream were torn between emerging Creole hypotheses on one hand and rapidly changing formal linguistic theories on the other. We have since come to learn that the historical hypotheses are not truly competing (see Fasold 1976). Debates among linguists during the 1970s focused substantially, and somewhat contentiously, on questions regarding the origin of AAVE, or how to include studies of linguistic variation in comprehensive (i.e., universal) linguistic theories.

Lorenzo Turner (1949) provided some of the strongest early evidence that linked Gullah to its African linguistic roots. Years later, Beryl Bailey (1965) was the first African American linguist to examine these issues in formal grammatical terms, and her work informed my comparative analyses of linguistic variation among Labov's Harlem informants (Baugh 1980), as well as the black adults whom I repeatedly interviewed in Los Angeles during the 1970s (Baugh 1983). By wonderful coincidence, Holm (1984) found grammatical variation in DeCamp's Jamaican Creole data that paralleled the linguistic variation that I had previously exposed in Labov's Harlem data and my own adult corpus from Los Angeles. In my case serendipity had more to do with historical implications than did any overt attempt to resolve the diachronic controversies that continue to capture the interest of growing numbers of linguists working on this topic.

Green (1998), Guy et al. (1996), and Mufwene et al. (1998) provide some of the most advanced analyses on this subject. In each of the preceding cases the authors devised expanded modes of analysis to capture linguistic and analytic nuances that were previously unknown. Rickford et al. (1991) overcame important methodological discrepancies found in earlier studies, and their analyses set the stage for McWorter's (1993) research regarding the grammatical significance of the serial verbs in the evolution of AAVE and related Creoles. Winford's (1992) analyses also advanced this line of research through more sophisticated integration of formal linguistic theory. Despite these welcome advances, the historical debate is far from being resolved, based substantially on new studies by linguists who study Canadian black English (Poplack and Tagliamonte 1989, 1991).

Working with other African American texts, including Botkin's ex-slave narratives, Bailey and Maynor (1987), Montgomery and Bailey (1987), and Schneider (1996) add to the historical depth of AAVE studies. The ex-slave narratives represent some of the oldest recordings of former slaves, and they have been used to help fill in some of the missing pieces of evidence for AAVE. Here too we find controversy, because many scholars disagree about fundamental aspects of spoken utterances and other linguistic content on these well-worn recordings. Edwards (1990) has produced some of the most advanced studies of phonetic differentiation between black and white speech.

Turning to contemporary usage, Smitherman's (1977) *Talkin' and Testifyin'* was among the first books on AAVE from a black cultural perspective. She provided one of the most vivid ethnolinguistic accounts of AAVE through an interdisciplinary perspective that was mindful of the constant linguistic tug-of-war faced by black people, who, as minority descendants of former slaves, take pride in African contributions to American culture. More recently she has published a comprehensive glossary of terms in a book titled *Black Talk* (Smitherman 1994), which includes an informative introduction regarding the evolution of vernacular African American dialects (see Folb 1980).

At present there are new and exciting technical linguistic studies of AAVE that, while not resolving all controversies, have nevertheless focused considerable scholarly attention on rigorous accounts of AAVE and historically related speech communities in the United States, Canada, the Caribbean, and Africa. Green's (1993) studies are especially noteworthy for their contribution to formal semantic analyses of AAVE, and Weldon (1996) has advanced our understanding of AAVE negative concord through sophisticated linguistic analyses that are much more compatible with contemporary linguistic theories; the list of other noteworthy contributions could go on at length.

Historical aspects of AAVE were central to studies by Creole scholars, which include Singler's (1991) studies of Liberian English, Patrick's (1995a, 1995b) extensive studies of Jamaican Creole, and Holm's (1984, 1991) comprehensive surveys of Caribbean Creoles, among others (see Ewers 1996). Hannah (1996) built on the pioneering work of Poplack and Sankoff (1987), who first observed historical linkages between Samana English and black American English from the Philadelphia area. Rickford (1996) added yet another layer to this debate through comparative analyses of African American populations in Jamaica and the United States. His conclusions— including documented patterns of population growth and migration among blacks—cast doubt on some prevailing historical interpretations. Those with strong historical interests would be well advised to consult the original studies for more complete details. Let it suffice to say that linguistic analyses of AAVE represent a robust and growing field of exciting intellectual inquiry.

EDUCATIONAL FOUNDATIONS FOR THE STUDY OF AAVE

A wave of educational research that focused on the linguistic welfare of African American students also flourished during the Civil Rights movement. Although segregated schools were outlawed in Brown v. Board (1953), the racial gap in academic performance has not significantly closed since then, and the linguistic consequences of slavery on American education have never been adequately reconciled. As part of President Johnson's war on poverty, a war yet to be won, several educational studies were sponsored to help identify various causes associated with the perpetual pattern of low academic achievement among black students.

Linguists who were instrumental in this venture included Torrey (1972), Shuy (1964), and Baratz and Shuy (1969), each of whom focused on ways to improve reading and literacy. Simpkins, Holt, and Simpkins (1974) elevated this effort through their cross-cultural reading program called "Bridge," which is being revived by Smitherman and Labov, based on the recognition that AAVE students must gradually learn standard English norms if they hope to succeed academically. Despite every good intention associated with these efforts, the earliest ventures focused on structural linguistic considerations; that is, they attempted to expose dialect differences between AAVE and SE. Since in earlier times relatively little was known about AAVE, educators and linguists devoted primary attention to dialect specification, which was impaired by considerable historical speculation.

Although those first deciphering steps were necessary, they were not sufficient to overcome the legacy of educational apartheid, and a central reason for this limitation grew from the fact that many black students did not want to "act white" (see Fordham and Ogbu 1985). This was especially true at a time when black nationalism and growing cultural pride were emerging, along with the ascendancy of the Black Panthers and the Nation of Islam. For those blacks who valued loyalty to African American culture, efforts by linguists and educators to unlock the gates to standard English were often met with skepticism, if not open resistance and hostility.

Some inner-city educators have developed strategies to help African American students navigate the linguistic maze toward academic success. Some schools in DeKalb County, Georgia, and south-central Los Angeles have developed special programs designed for AAVE students to help them toward proficient bidialectalism. Sledd (1969) observed an antiblack bias in his article titled "The Politics of Bidialectalism," thereby creating an educational double standard. He acknowledged that many white students were not obligated to learn AAVE as a second dialect. Learning another dialect can be an extremely difficult task, even for those who are highly motivated. A comparable dialect barrier exists when Americans attempt to produce British English as a secondary dialect; most attempts fall far short of fluency. SE fluency is, nevertheless, the appropriate and formidable objective of many programs for AAVE students. These bidialectalism programs tend to be pragmatic, recognizing strong institutionalized bias against AAVE and those who speak it. Although it makes little sense to formally teach AAVE to SE speakers (which rap and hip-hop already do to some extent through radio and television), there is an absolute need for greater social acceptance of linguistic diversity, including greater acceptance of a black accent.

Within the context of the competitive global economy, the linguistic diversity embodied throughout the American population is an underutilized resource. The educational implications of squandered linguistic assets have been politicized within debates on the value of bilingual education and growing legal and illegal immigration to the United States. AAVE students continue to fall between the policy cracks regarding the education of minority-language students (see Chapters 5 and 10), and it is for this reason that we find educators resorting to a host of strategies to increase SE proficiency among AAVE students. Few programs are designed to instill greater linguistic acceptance of citizens who lack SE proficiency.

English composition teachers have faced similar issues with the teaching of writing, and Shaughnessy's (1977) *Errors and Expectations* provides a classical introduction to the problems that English teachers confront as they attempt to teach prescribed writing standards to students who speak nonstandard English, or students who are in the midst of learning English as a secondary language.

In the final analysis, the linguistic demands of multifarious occupations vary considerably, and comprehensive educational strategies must move beyond ineffective practices of the past that have relegated language minority students to remedial classes in special education. Levin's philosophy of academic acceleration holds great appeal in this regard, because minority students cannot compete with traditional students if curricula are decelerated through extensive remediation. Language arts instruction should honor the linguistic heritage of every student at the same time that students are provided with adequate instruction that allows them to fulfill any professional ambition that is within their personal capacity to achieve.

ANTHROPOLOGICALLY ORIENTED STUDIES OF AAVE

Mitchell-Kernan (1971) offered yet another perspective on African American styles of communication, and her work revealed some important sexual differences in speaking styles. In a field of intellectual inquiry that had a strong bias in favor of male analysts, fieldworkers, and informants, she provided insights from a woman's point of view. Her studies moved beyond the purely structural considerations that had preoccupied linguists, and explored many of the social and anthropological issues that confronted diverse populations of black people.

Her work stood apart from studies by Abrahams (1974) and Kochman (1981), who concentrated on the language and stylistic repertoire of adolescent-to-adult black men. Taken collectively, these anthropologically oriented studies place their linguistic observations within the cultural tapestry of the vernacular African American community, albeit with primary emphasis on urban life.

Much of what we know today about ritualized insults and other African American speech acts derives specifically from anthropological work that tried to convey a sense of the daily lives and pressures that influence ordinary black folks who struggle with poverty. Their work exposed the verbal art of hustlin, rappin, and jive-talkin that still thrives today. Epic poems, toasts, boasts, and verbal jousting in various forms remain central to the work of anthropologists in African American communities, and their studies allow us to trace the evolution of changing linguistic norms among black people.

Kochman's (1981) *Black and White Styles in Conflict* served to illustrate the ways in which communication across racial lines breaks down and how differences in cultural orientation can lead to conflicts and violence. He provided several vivid examples of ways in which whites and blacks simply misinterpreted the same sociolinguistic episode, as well as the consequences of that misinterpretation. Goodwin's (1990) book titled *He Said, She Said* moves beyond analyses of single linguistic episodes and begins to track the consequences of rumor and innuendo in the self-serving retellings of stories among youthful African American friends and acquaintances. While most American teenagers engage in various forms of gossip, this practice is not only ritualized in the black community, it is also linked intricately to one's status in the peer group. Those who know the gossip, those who convey the gossip, and those who are the object of the gossip represent different interchangeable participants in this ritualized discourse. Goodwin's studies are all the more important because of her ability to gain access to this *semi-confidential* speech; while gossip—by definition—is not confidential, it is certainly mitigated and intended for a restricted audience. Moreover, that audience is being entrusted to protect the source of that gossip, although the evolving chain of gossip could lead to open conflict, hostility, or violence as rumors circulate.

The private discourse of *He Said, She Said* is shrouded in comparison to the public poetry of rappers and hip-hop artists who pride themselves on verbal mastery of AAVE as a sign of their legitimacy to talk about life in the ghetto. As Morgan (1998) observes, for every rap artist who signs a recording contract, there are hundreds, if not thousands, of aspiring African American poets who seek similar recognition. But there is a paradox confronting matters of authenticity, that is, distinguishing those who are real from those who ain't. Too much media exposure can diminish—from the black perspective—the credibility of rappers or hip-hop artists. Once they cross over and are discovered by white audiences, their esteem with former black devotees can plummet. The explanation for this is fairly straightforward: hip-hop that is real comes from the core of the inner city. Artists who have achieved sufficiently high levels of success consequently acquire enough wealth that they are perceived to be out of touch with their black constituents, with noteworthy exceptions where highly visible performers find themselves in conflict with the police or some other institutionalized authority. The essential point, however, is that rap and hip-hop are recent renditions of the African American oral tradition that has thrived since slavery. The significant difference at present lies in the marketability of the controversial lyrics that have become political fodder.

Thus far our anthropological review has concentrated on linguistic studies, that is, direct analyses of African American language in different circumstances. Ogbu's (1978) studies of castelike minorities in the United States are not focused on language per se, nor do they rely on racial classification; his work attempts to sort out differences between the various groups that reside in America, and he identifies three primary groups as follows:

> Our comparative study has led us to classify minority groups into (1) autonomous, (2) immigrant or voluntary, and (3) castelike or involuntary minorities.
> 1. Autonomous minorities are people who are minorities primarily in a numerical sense. American examples are Jews, Mormons, and the Amish. There are no non-White autonomous minorities in the United States. . . .
> 2. Immigrant or voluntary minorities are people who have moved more or less voluntarily to the United States—or any other society—because they desire more economic well-being, better overall opportunities, and/or greater political freedom. . . .
> 3. Castelike or involuntary minorities are people who were originally brought into the United States or any other society against their will. For example, through slavery, conquest, colonization or forced labor. Thereafter, these minorities were often relegated to menial positions and denied true assimilation into the mainstream society. . . . (Ogbu 1992, 8)

By combining Ogbu's categories without designated linguistic divisions, we create a grid that can be used to identify different sociolinguistic vantage points for every resident in the United States, and with slight modification this model could be adapted to other advanced industrialized societies that are dominated by a highly prescriptive standard language.

LINGUISTIC SELF-DIAGNOSIS AND SOCIOLINGUISTIC RELATIVITY

Figure 20 classifies three immigrant groups, by SE, SENN, and ENN, into nine categories I/IX. There are a host of other categories that one might consider, such as sex, or education, or access to technology, but for the sake of illustration our discussion is limited to nine basic heuristic categories (see Figure 20).

Please select the roman numeral that best represents your own language acquisition, that is, into which numerical category were you born? It is also important for you to compare your present status to your birth category. Has your sociolinguistic circumstance changed since you were born,

FIGURE 20.   Nonracial heuristic classification for individual linguistic relativity. Based on Ogbu's (1978, 1992) immigrant classification.

	Voluntary	Autonomous	Castelike or involuntary
SE *(Standard English is native)*	I	II	III
SENN *(Standard English is not native)*	IV	V	VI
ENN *(English is not native)* (See Fig. 3)	VII	VIII	IX

and, if so, what is the direction of that change? If your sociolinguistic status has not changed since birth, then you are maintaining the linguistic legacy of your ancestors. However, if your category has ever changed, then so too has your sociolinguistic status. In every instance of individual change, you have—for very personal reasons—come to occupy a category that your forebears did not. Why? What influenced this change, or lack of linguistic change?

Although politicians are fond of referring to "the American people," seeking to imply cohesive homogeneity, the true reality of sociolinguistic heterogeneity within the United States is portrayed in Figure 20. It is also important to note that the American population is not equally distributed throughout these categories, and I have described these concepts elsewhere in "econolinguistic" terms (Baugh 1996). Be that as it may, this exercise is directed at you—the reader. Your linguistic heritage inevitably plays a significant role in how you view linguistic diversity. However, linguistic diversity has always been a by-product of the American heritage.

Your sociolinguistic status, based on your own diagnosis, is also likely to determine your relative (de)valuation of immigration: do you welcome the newest wave of American immigrants, or not? This issue is not unique to the United States; similar models could be devised for other advanced industrialized nations, particularly those where immigration is controversial. Postcolonial nations where slavery once thrived share a special burden, based on their (in)ability to demonstrate the collective sociopolitical will to truly overcome discrimination against slave descendants by eliminating the host of barriers—in housing, education, employment, access to high-quality medical care, access to a high-quality legal defense, etc.—that were once legally denied to slaves.

IMPLICATIONS FOR FUTURE
INTERDISCIPLINARY RESEARCH

As previously indicated, this review is not comprehensive. I have said nothing of the important scholarship that has been produced by communication scholars, including those who study communication disorders (Seymour and Seymour 1981; Stockman 1986, 1996; Champion 1995; Wyatt 1996; Kamhi, Pollock, and Harris 1996), nor did I go into greater detail regarding efforts among English teachers and civil-rights attorneys who acknowledge the linguistic difficulties that confront speakers of AAVE in a society that has grown weary of debates over Ebonics and racially mandated affirmative action programs.

Politicians in California and elsewhere reacted to the Ebonics controversy with a flurry of legislation to ban funding for such programs, particularly if they claim bilingual legitimacy. However, denying bilingual funding to black students (which may be understandable) does nothing to advance their standard English proficiency, and it is this more daunting educational task that has somehow been overlooked by the policy makers and educational reformers who are directly responsible for the educational welfare of less-fortunate students.

It is my hope that the linguistic contribution to the eventual elimination of racism comes through instilling greater acceptance of linguistic diversity, not merely greater tolerance of group differences. After all, linguistic heterogeneity is an obvious artifact of America's precolonial and postcolonial history, first conveyed through hundreds of indigenous languages that eventually declined under relentless waves of immigration and corresponding tides of linguistic change.

Descendants of former slaves have typically fared less well than have most voluntary immigrants, and the ultimate test of American equality, which is embodied in the ethic that hard work and fair play will lead to a personally rewarding life, lies in our honest acknowledgment of the extent to which children born into categories IV through IX in Figure 20 are indeed able to change their personal circumstances for the better. Greater social equality is more likely to ensure the positive engagement of citizens who share legacies of being socially disenfranchised. Once equal opportunities come to prevail, then—and only then—will America achieve her cherished colorblind ambition.

Notes

Chapter Two

1. Farrell ignores cultural and economic factors as a determinant of IQ scores. Yet, as we have seen, even Bloomfield was aware that whether one is "privileged" or "less fortunate" is a major determining factor in academic success. Furthermore, the same black students who get low scores on standardized IQ tests score much higher on the alternative tests developed by black psychologists that are biased in favor of black culture.

2. Readers who are unfamiliar with the history of this thesis are encouraged to read Farrell (1978, 1983, 1984a, 1984b). Detailed commentary on Farrell's hypotheses can be found in Greenberg 1984, Hartwell 1984, Himley 1984, and Stratton 1984. Sledd (1983, 1984) and Farrell (1984b) debate the pedagogical dimensions of the hypotheses.

3. Thomas Sebeok, in the course of a lecture on the history of communication presented at the University of Texas at Austin, stressed the history of "meta-tool" making as a uniquely human behavior which represents further evidence of detailed abstract thought among preliterate humans. While humans are not the only species to make tools, they are the only meta-tool makers. There is substantial archeological evidence to support the early existence of meta-tools among all races prior to the classical period in Greece. Such meta-tools are created for the express purpose of producing other tools; one must produce a meta-tool in order to make the tool that is desired.

Chapter Five

1. Educational malpraxis refers to the entire range and combination of maladies that may foster educational negligence by professional educators. *Malpractice* refers specifically to the work of trained professionals, but *malpraxis* is

intended to be more comprehensive, including misconduct, malfeasance, malpractice, and all other forms of professional negligence.

2. According to Culhane (1992), educators concerned with this issue, that is, the teaching of standard English to SENN students, might explore options through the Individuals with Disabilities Education Act (Education of the Handicapped) and the new flexibility in Title I programs that give schools and school districts tremendous latitude in the creation of innovative programs for students in poverty. Drawing on experience from the black English trial, care should be taken not to equate pathological linguistic disabilities with socially grounded linguistic disadvantages suffered by those who do not speak (or write) standard English.

3. Doctors may see x number of patients per hour, and may work y hours per day. Teachers may see a number of students per class and may have b classes per day. In much the same manner that a medical advisory board might inform a doctor that (s)he is seeing too many patients per hour, so too might an educational advisory committee suggest that a given teacher is burdened by having to teach too many students per day. The doctor who sees too many patients is, perhaps, more likely to commit acts of malpractice than might be a comparable doctor who sees fewer patients. Similarly, a teacher who teaches a large class or several large classes may be more likely to commit acts of malpractice that might otherwise be avoided with smaller classes, or with improved strategies on how to effectively manage large classes.

4. Corporations and businesses occasionally share their staff and resources with (local) educators. In many instances this takes the form of shared personnel, where a member of the corporate or business community comes to the school for brief to extended periods of time. They are called upon to impart knowledge to students based on their professional experience. In my opinion the time is long overdue for corporations and businesses to recognize the potential value of reciprocal exchange programs.

Based on my lifelong experience with teachers, businesses and corporations would do well to find one, or two, or three, local teachers who have a history of success under difficult conditions. Good teachers at inner-city schools have been "downsized" far longer than have their softer counterparts in the affluent private sector. Schools were lean and mean long before corporations knew they were on a collision course with stringent fiscal measures. In much the same manner that schools have called on corporations to lend support through shared personnel, businesses could hire teachers as consultants to help trim their fat and guide them toward the high levels of professional productivity that so many good teachers embody.

Chapter Six

1. *Black English* (New York: Random House, 1972).
2. Results from a study by G. Richard Tucker and Wallace E. Lambert

support this position. See "White and Negro Listeners' Reactions to Various American-English Dialects" in Fishman (1972).

Chapter Eight

1. I have adopted the term *American slave descendants* (ASD) for two reasons. First, this discussion looks at terms of self-reference, and ASD strives for terminological neutrality in a text that must refer to Americans with African ancestors. The second justification grows from Edmund Morris's self-identification as an "African American." Morris is a naturalized American, and a white native of Kenya. In an article entitled "Just 'Americans'" in the *Washington Post,* 12 February 1989, he labeled himself as an "African American" in order to mock Jesse Jackson's plea. Morris cannot claim to be a descendant of American slavery, and the adopted terminology excludes people like him.

2. Not all American slave descendants are active members of VAAC. By *vernacular African American culture* I refer to the African American cultural traditions that have been developed in racial isolation from the majority culture. Some whites are active in VAAC, including many musicians, dancers, and teachers. Many ASD, on the other hand, have limited contact with VAAC. Thus, as we strive to identify the vernacular African American community, race and active participation in black culture are both taken into account.

3. Geneva Smitherman (1987) continues this tradition among scholars. She recognizes that "standard" English is a political construct, and as such it constitutes a dialect of wider communication. The term *standard* continues to convey a sense of linguistic legitimacy that is not afforded to dialects that are not valued by the majority culture. The type of renaming that she advocates is consistent with similar processes in VAAC.

4. The "Jackson factor" is employed here for expedience. As the only African American ever to mount a viable presidential campaign, his social influence is unique when compared with any other minority leader in America. This shorthand is discussed in more detail later in the text.

5. Black people commonly refer to each other as Brother or Sister as signs of racial solidarity. In this vein, I use the words here as terms of respect for fellow African American men and women.

6. I would like to thank Dr. Harold Luft, of the University of California, San Francisco Medical School, for his assistance; he provided advice and access to massive medical files that expedited the telephone survey. My survey combined the principles of judgment samples and random samples. In order to ensure that a representative population of diverse informants could be contacted, zip codes and telephone prefixes were aligned with census data, allowing for targeted surveys among rich, poor, white, and nonwhite informants. A total of 362 households were contacted before obtaining the sample of 300 subjects. The questions were asked of all who agreed to participate; parental permission was obtained prior to interviews with minors.

Chapter Nine

1. The situation regarding contracted *is* (i.e., /s/) is moot because of phonological neutralization; "He's steady. . . ." would sound identical to "He steady. . . ."

Chapter Ten

1. As an African American scholar and man I face a special methodological paradox when analyzing AAVE, because I do have linguistic intuitions about my native dialect. However, as a linguist, I am also familiar with analyses of these forms, to say nothing of the fact that my academic training has bombarded me with exposure to SE, and I no longer feel that my intuitions about AAVE should serve as the "best evidence" on this subject. Despite this observation, I am not fanatical on this point; my intuitions have helped me at various stages of analyses, particularly in the formulation of relevant questionnaires.

2. Ms. Kathy Lewis is a native Texan. Her ancestors were slaves in Central Texas and she has close relatives and friends who live in rural and urban areas near Austin. Her assistance has been a tremendous asset to the success of this research.

3. I would like to thank Keith Walters for pointing out this shared usage to me. When I first began this study I assumed that semi-auxiliary *come* was unique to AAVE. As suggested by other linguistic comparisons of AAVE and SVE, the historical implications are apparent, even if they tend to be somewhat moot due to sparse or questionable documentation in critical cases, like the present observations.

Glossary

AAVE: African American vernacular English
AFDC: Aid to Families with Dependent Children
ASD: American slave descendants
Creole: A new native language born of two or more languages in contact (*see* pidgin)
ENN: English not native
ERIC: Education Research Information Clearinghouse
ESL: English as second language
HPE: Hawaiian pidgin English
LSA: Linguistic Society of America
pidgin: The linguistic product of contact between two or more languages that has no native speakers.
SE: Standard English
SENN: Standard English is not native
SEP: Standard English proficiency program
Special Education: Federal-to-local educational programs for children with disabilities
SVE: Southern vernacular English
Title I: Federal education programs for children in poverty
Title VII: Federal funding for local educational programs for language minority students.
VAAC: Vernacular African American culture

References

Abrahams, R. D. (1974). "Black Talking on the Streets." In R. Bauman and J. Sherzer (eds.), *Explorations in the Ethnography of Speaking,* pp. 240–262. Cambridge: Cambridge University Press.

Abramson, A. S. (1979). "The Noncategorical Perception of Tone Categories in Thai." In Björn Lindblom and Sven Öhman (eds.), *Frontiers of Speech Communication Research,* pp. 127–134. New York: Academic Press.

Bailey, Beryl. (1965). "Toward a New Perspective in Negro English Dialectology." *American Speech* 40: 171–177.

Bailey, Guy. (1987). "Are Black and White Vernaculars Diverging?" *American Speech* 62: 32–39.

Bailey, Guy, and Maynor, N. (1987). "Decreolization?" *Language in Society,* 16: 449–473.

Ball, A. (1991). *Organizational Patterns in the Oral and Written Expository Language of African American Adolescents.* Ph.D. diss., Stanford University.

Ball, Arnetha. (1992). "Cultural Preference and the Expository Writing of African-American Adolescents." *Written Communication* 9: 501–532.

———. (1995). "Investigating Language, Learning, and Linguistic Competence of African-American Children: Torrey Revisited." *Linguistics and Education* 7: 23–46.

Banks, J. (1994). *Multiethnic Education: Theory and Practice.* Boston: Allyn and Bacon.

Baratz, J. C., and Shuy, R. W. (1969). *Teaching Black Children to Read.* Washington, D.C.: Center for Applied Linguistics

Baugh, B. (1994). *Learning Partners: Helping Children and Parents Learn Together.* Thousand Oaks, Calif.: Learning Partners, Inc.

Baugh, J. (1980). "A Reexamination of the Black English Copula." In William

Labov (ed.), *Locating Language in Space and Time,* pp. 83–106. Orlando, Fla.: Academic Press.

———. (1981). "Design and Implementation of Writing Instruction for Speakers of Non-Standard English: Perspectives for a National Neighborhood Literacy Program." In Bruce Cronnell (ed.), *The Writing Needs of Linguistically Different Students.* Los Alamitos, Calif.: SWRL Educational Research and Development.

———. (1983). *Black Street Speech: Its History, Structure, and Survival.* Austin: University of Texas Press.

———. (1984). "Steady: Progressive Aspect in Black English." *American Speech* 50: 3–12.

———. (1988). "Language and Race: Some Implications for Linguistic Science." In. F. Newmeyer (ed.), *Linguistics: The Cambridge Survey.* Vol. 4, pp. 64–74. Cambridge: Cambridge University.

———. (1996). "Dimensions of a Theory of Econolinguistics." In Gregory R. Guy et al. (eds.), *Towards a Social Science of Language: Volume 1: Variation and Change in Language in Society,* pp. 397–419.

———. (1997). "What's in a Name? That by Which We Call the Linguistic Consequences of the African Slave Trade." *The Quarterly of the National Writing Project* 19: 9.

———. (1998). "Linguistics, Education, and the Law: Educational Reform for African-American Language Minority Students." In S. Mufwene et al. (eds.), *African American English: Structure, History, and Usage,* pp. 282–301. London: Routledge.

Bennett, Lerone, Jr. (1967). "What's in a Name?" *Ebony* 23 (Nov. 1967): 46–48, 50–52, 54.

Bennett, William J. (1986). *What Works: Research about Teaching and Learning.* Washington, D.C.: U.S. Department of Education.

Binkley, Marilyn R., et al. (1986). *Becoming a Nation of Readers: Implications for Teachers.* Washington, D.C.: U.S. Department of Education, Office of Educational Research and Improvement.

Binnick, Robert I. (1971). "Bring and Come." *Linguistic Inquiry* 11: 260–265.

Blom, J. P., and Gumperz, J. J. (1972). "Social Meaning in Linguistic Structure: Code-Switching in Norway." In John J. Gumperz and Dell Hymes (eds.), *Directions in Sociolinguistics,* pp. 207–238. New York: Holt, Rinehart & Winston.

Bloomfield, Leonard. (1933). *Language.* London: Allen & Unwin.

Boas, Franz. (1940). *Race, Language and Culture.* New York: The Free Press.

Bobo, Lawrence. (1983). "Whites' Opposition to Busing: Symbolic Racism or Realistic Group Conflict?" *Journal of Personality and Social Psychology* 45: 1196–1210.

Bortoni, Stella. (1985). *Urbanization of Rural Dialect Speakers: A Sociolinguistic Study in Brazil.* Cambridge: Cambridge University Press.

Brewer, J. (1986). "Durative Marker or Hypercorrection? The Case of -s in the WPA Ex-Slave Narratives." In M. Montgomery and G. Bailey (eds.), *Language Variety in the South,* pp. 131–148. Montgomery: University of Alabama Press.

Bridges, Edward. (1992). *The Incompetent Teacher.* Philadelphia: Falmer Press.

Brown, R., and Gilman, A. (1960). "The Pronouns of Power and Solidarity." In Thomas Sebeok (ed.), *Style in Language,* pp. 235–276. Cambridge, Mass.: MIT Press.

Brown, P., and Levinson, S. (1978). "Universals of Language Usage: Politeness Phenomena." In E. Goody (ed.), *Questions and Politeness Strategies in Social Interaction.* Cambridge: Cambridge University Press.

Brown v. Board of Education, 347 U.S. 483, 493 (1954).

Carnoy, Martin. (1994). *Faded Dreams.* Cambridge: Cambridge University Press.

Cazden, C., Johns, V., and Hymes, D. (eds.). (1972). *Functions of Language in the Classroom.* New York: Teachers College Press.

Chafe, Wallace (ed.). (1980). *The Pear Stories: Cognitive, Cultural, and Linguistics Aspects of Narrative Production.* Norwood , N.J.: Ablex.

Chambers, John. (1983). *Black English: Educational Equity and the Law.* Ann Arbor: Karoma Press.

Champion, Tempii. (1995). "A Description of Narrative Production and Development in Child Speakers of African American English." Ph.D. diss. University of Massachusetts, Amherst.

Chomsky, Noam. (1965). *Aspects of a Theory of Syntax.* Cambridge, Mass.: MIT Press.

———. (1977). *Language and Responsibility.* New York: Pantheon Books.

Chomsky, Noam, and Halle, Morris. (1968). *The Sound Patterns of English.* Harper and Row.

Clark, Eve. (1974). "Normal States and Evaluative Viewpoints." *Language* 50: 316–332.

Conant, James B. (1961). *Slums and Suburbs.* New York: Signet.

Culhane, J. G. (1992). "Reinvigorating Educational Malpractice Claims: A Representational Focus." *Washington Law Review* 67: 2, 349–414.

Darling-Hammond, Linda. (1994). "National Standards and Assessments: Will They Improve Education?" *American Journal of Education* 102: 478–510.

DeCamp, David. (1971). "Hypercorrection and Rule Generalization." *Language in Society* 1: 87–90.

Delpit, L. (1986). "Skills and Other Dilemmas of a Progressive Black Educator." *Harvard Educational Review* 56: 379–385.

———. (1988). "The Silenced Dialogue: Power and Pedagogy in Educating Other People's Children." *Harvard Educational Review* 58: 280–298.

Dewey, J. (1938). *Experience and Education.* New York: Macmillan.

Dillard, J. L. (1972). *Black English.* New York: Random House.

DuBois, W. E. B. (1928). "The Name 'Negro.'" *The Crisis* 35: 96–97.

Edwards, Walter. (1990). "Phonetic Differentiation between Black and White Speech in East-Side Detroit." *Word* 41: 203–218.

Elmore, R. F., and Fuhrman, S. H. (1993). "Opportunity to Learn and the State Role in Education." In S. L. Traiman (ed.), *The Debate on Opportunity-to-Learn Standards: Supporting Works,* pp. 73–102. Washington, D.C.: National Governors Association.

Emmett, Kathleen, and Machamer, Peter. (1976). *Perception: An Annotated Bibliography.* New York: Garland.

Ewers, Traute. (1996). *The Origin of American Black English: Be-Forms in the HOODOO Texts.* Berlin: Mouton de Gruyter.

Fairbaugh, Glenn, and Davis, Kenneth E. (1988). "Trends in Antiblack Prejudice, 1972–1984: Region and Cohort Effects." *American Journal of Sociology* 94: 251–272.

Farrell, Thomas. (1983). "IQ and Standard English." *College Composition & Communication* 34: 470–484.

———. (1984a). "Reply by Thomas J. Farrell." *College Composition and Communication* 35: 469–478.

———. (1984b). "Comment on James Sledd's 'In Defense of the Students' Right.'" *College English* 46: 821–822.

Fasold, Ralph. (1972). *Tense Marking in Black English.* Washington, D.C.: Center for Applied Linguistics.

———. (1976). "One Hundred Years from Syntax to Phonology." In Sanford B. Steever, Carol A. Walder, and Salikoko S. Mufwene (eds.), *Papers from the Parasession on Diachronic Syntax,* pp. 79–87. Chicago: Chicago Linguistic Society.

Ferguson, C. A. (1959). "Diglossia." *Word* 15: 325–340.

Fillmore, Charles, J. (1966). "Deictic Categories in the Semantics of 'Come.'" *Foundations of Language* 2: 219–227.

Fishman, Joshua. (1972a). *Readings in the Sociology of Language.* The Hague: Mouton.

———. (1972b). *Advances in the Sociology of Language.* Vol. II. The Hague: Mouton.

———. (1991). *Reversing Language Shift: Theoretical and Empirical Foundations of Assistance to Threatened Languages.* Clevedon, England: Multilingual Matters.

Flaster, D. J. (1983). *Malpractice.* New York: Scribner.

Flexner, Stuart B. (1976). *I Hear America Talking: An Illustrated Treasury of American Words and Phrases.* New York: Van Nostrand.

Folb, Edith. 1980. *Runnin' Down Some Lines.* Cambridge, Mass.: Harvard University Press.

Fordham, Signithia, and Ogbu, John. (1985). "Black Students' School Success:

Coping with the Burden of 'Acting White'." *The Urban Review* 18: 176–206.

Foster, Michele. (1997). "Ebonics and All That Jazz: Cutting through the Politics of Linguistics Education and Race." *The Quarterly of the National Writing Project* 19: 7–12.

Gal, Susan. (1978). "Peasant Men Can't Get Wives." *Language in Society* 7: 1–16.

Galindo, Letticia. (1995). "Language Attitudes toward Spanish and English Varieties: A Chicano Perspective." *Hispanic Journal of Behavioral Sciences* 17: 77–99.

Gardner, H. (1991). *The Unschooled Mind.* New York: Basic Books.

———. (1993). *Frames of Mind.* New York: Basic Books.

Gee. J. (1990). *Social Linguistics and Literacies.* London: Falmer Press.

Giles, Howard. (1979). "Ethnicity Markers in Speech." In Klaus Scherer and Howard Giles (eds.), *Social Markers in Speech,* pp. 251–289. Cambridge: Cambridge University Press.

Giles, Howard, and Powesland, Peter. (1975). *Speech Styles and Social Evaluation.* New York: Academic Press.

Goffman, Erving. (1959). *The Presentation of Self in Everyday Life.* New York: Anchor.

———. (1972). "The Neglected Situation." In Pier P. Giglioli (ed.), *Language in Social Contexts,* pp. 61–66. New York: Penguin.

Goodwin, Marjorie Harness. (1990). *He-Said-She-Said: Talk as Social Organization among Black Children.* Bloomington: Indiana University Press.

Green, Lisa. (1993). Topics in African American English: The Verb System Analysis. Ph.D. diss., University of Massachusetts, Amherst.

———. (1995). Study of Verb Classes in African American English. *Linguistics and Education* 7, 65–82.

———. (1998). "Aspect and Predicate Phrases in African-American Vernacular English." In Salikoko Mufwene et al. (eds.), *African American English: Structure, History, and Usage,* pp. 37–68. London: Routledge.

Greenberg, K. (1984). "Response No. 1 to Thomas J. Farrell." *College Composition and Communication* 35: 461–465.

Guy, Gregory R. Feagin; Crawford-Schiffrin, Deborah; and Baugh, John (eds.). (1996). *Towards a Social Science of Language: Volume 1: Variation and Change in Language and Society.* Philadelphia: John Benjamins.

Hakuta, Kenji, et al. (1994). *Bilingual Education and Policy Reform.* Final Report from the Carnegie Foundation Study Group. Stanford University School of Education.

Hannah, Dawn. (1996). "Copula Absence in Samaná English." Ph.D. qualifying paper, Department of Linguistics, Stanford University.

Hartwell, P. (1984). "Response No. 3 to Thomas J. Farrell." *College Composition and Communication* 35:461–465.

Haugen, Einar. (1972). *The Ecology of Language.* Stanford, Calif.: Stanford University Press.

Heath, S. B. (1983). *Ways with Words: Language, Life, and Work in Communities and Classrooms.* Cambridge: Cambridge University Press.

Heath, S. B., and McLaughlin, M. (eds.). (1993). *Identity and Inner-City Youth: Beyond Ethnicity and Gender.* New York: Teachers College Press.

Himley, M. (1984). "Response No. 3 to Thomas J. Farrell." *College Composition and Communication* 35:461–465.

Hollins, Etta; King, Joyce E.; and Hayman, Warren C. (eds.). (1994). *Teaching Diverse Populations: Formulating a Knowledge Base.* Albany: SUNY Press.

Holm, J. (1984). "Variability of the Copula in Black English and Its Creole Kin." *American Speech* 59: 291–309.

———. (1991). "The Atlantic Creoles and the Language of the Ex-Slave Recordings." In Guy Bailey, Natalie Maynor, and Patricia Cukor-Avila (eds.), *The Emergence of Black English,* pp. 231–248. Philadelphia: John Benjamins.

Hoover, Mary. (1978). "Community Attitudes toward Black English." *Language in Society* 7:65–87.

Hoover, Mary; McNair-Knox, Faye; Lewis, Shirley A. R.; and Politzer, Robert L. (1996). "Testing African American Children." In *Handbook of Test Measurement for Black Populations,* edited by Reginald L. Jones. Vol. 1, pp. 383–393. Hampton, Va.: Cobb & Henry.

Hymes, D. (ed.). (1964). *Language in Culture and Society.* New York: Harper and Row.

Jensen, A. (1969). "How Much Can We Boost IQ and Scholastic Achievement?" *Harvard Educational Review* 39: 1–123.

Kamhi, Alan G.; Pollock, Karen E.; and Harris, Joyce L. (eds). (1996). *Communication Development and Disorders in African American Children: Research, Assessment, and Intervention.* Baltimore: Brookes.

Kerr-Mattox, Beverly J. (1987). "Teacher Attitudes toward Black English." M.A. thesis: Texas A&M University.

Kochman, Thomas. (1981). *Black and White Styles in Conflict.* Chicago: University of Chicago Press.

Kozol, J. (1991). *Savage Inequalities.* New York: Crown.

Kroch, A., and Labov, W. (1972). "Resolution in Response to Arthur Jensen (1969)." *Linguistic Society of America Bulletin* (March). Washington: Linguistic Society of America.

Labov, William. (1963). "The Social Motivation of Sound Change." *Word* 19: 273–309.

———. (1966). *The Social Stratification of English in New York City.* Washington, D.C.: Center for Applied Linguistics.

———. (1969a). "Contraction, Deletion, and Inherent Variability of the English Copula." *Language* 45: 715–762.

————. (1969b). "The Logic of Nonstandard English." In James Alatis (ed.), *Georgetown Monograph Series on Languages and Linguistics* 22: 1–44. Washington, D.C.: Georgetown University Press.

————. (1972a). *Language in the Inner-City: Studies in the Black English Vernacular.* Philadelphia: University of Pennsylvania Press.

————. (1972b). *Sociolinguistic Patterns.* Philadelphia: University of Pennsylvania Press.

————. (1982). "Objectivity and Commitment in Linguistic Science: The Case of the Black English Trial in Ann Arbor." *Language in Society* 11: 165–201.

————. (1994). *Principles of Linguistic Change: Internal Factors.* Oxford: Blackwell.

Labov, William; Cohen, Paul; Robins, Clarence; and Lewis, John. (1968). *A study of the Non-Standard English of Negro and Puerto Rican Speakers in New York City.* USOE Final Report. Research Project 3,288.

Labov, William, and Harris, Wendell. (1986). "De Facto Segregation of Black and White Vernaculars." In D. Sankoff (ed.), *Diversity and Diachrony,* pp. 1–24. Amsterdam: John Benjamins Publishing.

Ladson-Billings, G. (1995). *The Dreamkeepers.* San Francisco: Jossey-Bass.

Lakoff, Robin. (1974). "Remarks on This and That." *Chicago Linguistic Society* 10: 345–356.

Lee, C. (1995). A Culturally Based Cognitive Apprenticeship: Teaching African American High School Students Skills in Literary Interpretation. *Reading Research Quarterly* 30: 608–630.

Le Page, R. B., and Tabouret-Keller, Andrée. (1985). Acts of Identity: Creole-Based Approaches to Language and Ethnicity. Cambridge: Cambridge University Press.

Manes, Joan, and Wolfson, Nessa (eds.). (1985). *Language and Inequality.* Berlin: Mouton.

McLaughlin, Milbrey; Ire, Merit A.; and Hangman, Juliet. (1994). *Urban Sanctuaries: Neighborhood Organizations in the Lives and Futures of Inner-City Youth.* San Francisco: Jossey-Bass.

McWorter, John. (1993). *A New Model of Creole Genesis.* Ph.D. diss., Stanford University.

Milroy, Leslie. 1980. *Language and Social Networks.* Baltimore: University Park Press.

Milroy, James, and Milroy, Lesley (eds). (1993). *Real English: The Grammar of English Dialects in the British Isles.* London and New York: Longman.

Mitchell-Kernan, Claudia. (1969). *Language Behavior in a Black Urban Community.* Language-Behavior Laboratory Working Paper 23. Berkeley: University of California.

Montgomery, Michael, and Bailey, Guy. (1986). *Language Variety in the South.* Tuscaloosa: University of Alabama Press.

Morgan, Marcyliena. (1998). "More Than a Mood or an Attitude: Discourse and Verbal Genres in African-American Culture." In Salikoko Mufwene et al. (eds.), *African American English: Structure, History, and Usage,* pp. 251–281. London: Routledge.

Mufwene, Salikoko S. (1983). "Some Observations on the Verb in Black English Vernacular." Austin: University of Texas, African and Afro-American Studies Research Center. Working paper.

———. (1992). *Ideology and Facts on African American Vernacular English. Pragmatics* 2: 141–166.

Mufwene, Salikoko S.; Rickford, John; Bailey, Guy; and Baugh, John (eds.). (1998). *African American English: Structure, History, and Usage.* London: Routledge.

Myhill, John, and Harris, Wendell. (1986). "The Use of Verbal -s Inflection in BEV." In David Sankoff (ed.), *Diversity and Diachrony,* pp. 25–32. Amsterdam: John Benjamins.

Nunberg, Geoff. (1997). "Double Standards." *Natural Language and Linguistic Theory* 15 (4): 667–675.

Ogbu, J. (1978). *Minority Education and Caste.* New York: Academic Press.

———. (1992). "Understanding Cultural Diversity and Learning." *Educational Researcher,* November 5–14.

Ong, Walter. (1982). *Orality and Literacy: The Technologizing of the Word.* London: Routledge.

Orr, Elinor Wilson. (1987). *Twice as Less: Black English and the Performance of Black Students in Mathematics and Science.* New York: Norton.

Patrick, Peter. (1995a). "Recent Jamaican Words in Sociolinguistic Context." *American Speech* 70 (3): 227–264.

———. (1995b). "The Urbanization of Creole Phonology: Variation and Change in Jamaican (KYA)." In Gregory R. Guy, Crawford Feagin, Deborah Schiffrin, and John Baugh (eds.), *Towards a Social Science of Language: Papers in Honor of William Labov. Vol. 1, Variation and Change in Language and Society,* pp. 329–355. Amsterdam: John Benjamins.

Pinker, S. (1994). *The Language Instinct: How the Mind Creates Language.* New York: William Morrow.

Pitts, Walter. (1981). "Beyond Hypercorrection: The Use of Emphatic -z in BEV." *Chicago Linguistic Society* 17: 303–310.

———. (1986). "Contrastive Use of Verbal -z in Slave Narratives." In David Sankoff (ed.), *Diversity and Diachrony,* pp. 73–82. Amsterdam: John Benjamins.

Poplack, Shana. (1978). "Quantitative Analysis of Constraints on Code-Switching." New York: City University of New York, Centro de Estudios Puertorriqueños.

Poplack, Shana, and Tagliamonte, Sali. (1989). "There's No Tense Like the Present: Verbal -s Inflection in Early Black English." *Language Variation and Change* 1: 47–84.

Poplack, Shana, and Tagliamonte, Sali. (1991). "African American English in the Diaspora: Evidence from Old-Line Nova Scotians." *Language Variation and Change* 3: 301–39.

Poplack, Shana, and Sankoff, David. (1987). "The Philadelphia Story in the Spanish Caribbean." *American Speech* 63: 291–314.

Rafky, David M. (1970). "The Semantics of Negritude." *American Speech* 45: 30–44.

Rickford, John. (1975). "Carrying the New Wave into Syntax: The Case of Black English BIN." In Ralph Fasold and Roger Shuy (eds.), *Analyzing Variation in Language,* pp. 162–183. Washington, D.C.: Georgetown University Press.

———. (1986). "Social Contact and Linguistic Diffusion: Hiberno-English and New World Black English." *Language* 62: 245–289.

———. (1987). "Are Black and White Vernaculars Diverging?" *American Speech* 62: 55–61.

———. (1996). "Copula Variability in Jamaican Creole and African American Vernacular English: A Reanalysis of DeCamp's Texts." In Gregory R. Guy, Crawford Feagin, Deborah Schiffrin, and John Baugh (eds.), *Towards a Social Science of Language: Papers in Honor of William Labov. Vol. 1, Variation and Change in Language and Society,* pp. 357–372. Amsterdam: John Benjamins.

Rickford, John R.; Ball, A. F.; Blake, R.; Jackson, R.; and Martin, N. (1991). "Rappin' on the Copula Coffin: Theoretical and Methodological Issues in the Analysis of Copula Variation in African-American Vernacular English." *Language Variation and Change* 3(1): 103–132.

Rickford, J., and Rickford, A. (1995). "Dialect Readers Revisited." *Linguistics in Education* 7: 107–128.

Rodriguez, Richard. (1982) *Hunger of Memory: The Education of Richard Rodriguez.* New York: Bantam.

Rosch, Eleanor. (1973). "On the Internal Structure of Perceptual and Semantic Categories." In Timothy E. Moore (ed.), *Cognitive Development and the Acquisition of Language,* pp. 111–114. New York: Academic Press.

Sag, Ivan. (1973). "On the State and Progress of Progressives and Statives." In Charles-James N. Bailey and Roger W. Shuy (eds), *New Ways of Analyzing Variation in English,* pp. 83–95. Washington, D.C.: Georgetown University Press.

Sapir, Edward. (1921). *Language.* New York: Harcourt, Brace and World.

Schneider, Edgar. (1982). "On the History of Black English in the U.S.A.: Some New Evidence." *English World-Wide* 3: 18–46.

———, (ed.). (1996). *Varieties of English around the World: Focus on the USA.* Amsterdam: John Benjamins.

Sears, David O.; Hensler, Carl P.; and Speer, Leslie K. (1979). "Whites' Opposition to Busing: Self-Interest or Symbolic Politics?" *American Political Science Review* 73: 369–84.

Seymour, Harry N., and Seymour, Charlena M. (1981). "Black English and Standard American English Contrasts in Consonantal Development of Four and Five Year Old Children." *Journal of Speech and Hearing Disorders.* pp. 274–280.

Shaughnessy, Myna. (1977). *Errors and Expectations.* New York: Oxford University Press.

Shuman, Howard; Steeh, Charlotte; and Bobo, Lawrence. (1985). *Racial Attitudes in America: Trends and Interpretations.* Cambridge, Mass.: Harvard University Press.

Shulman, Judy (ed.). (1994). *Diversity in the Classroom.* Hillsdale, N.J.: Lawrence Erlbaum Associates.

Shulman, Lee S. (1987). "Knowledge and Teaching: Foundations of the New Reform." *Harvard Educational Review.* 57 (1): 1–22.

Shuy, Roger (ed.). (1964). *Social Dialects and Language Learning.* Champaign, Ill.: National Council of Teachers of English.

Simpkins, Gary, and Holt, Grace. (1977). *Bridge: A Cross-Cultural Reading Program.* Boston: Houghton Mifflin.

Singler, John Victor. (1991). "Copula Variation in Liberian Settler English and American Black English." In Walter F. Edwards and Donald Winford (eds.), *Verb Phrase Patterns in Black English and Creole,* pp. 129–164. Detroit: Wayne State University Press.

Sledd, James. (1969). "Bi-Dialectalism: The Linguistics of White Supremacy." *English Journal* pp. 1307–1329.

———. (1983). "In Defense of the Students' Right." *College English* 45: 667–675.

———. (1984). "James Sledd Responds." *College English* 46: 822–829.

Smith, Ernie. (1992). "African American Language Behavior: A World of Difference." In Philip H. Dryer (ed.), *Claremont Reading Conference,* pp. 39–53. Pomona: Claremont College.

———. (1997). "What Is Black English? What Is Ebonics?" In Theresa Perry and Lisa Delpit (eds.), *The Real Ebonics Debate: Power, Language, and the Education of African-American Children,* pp. 14–15. *Rethinking Schools.*

Smith, Marshall S., and O'Day, Jennifer. (1991). "Systemic School Reform." In S. Fuhrman and B. Malen (eds.), *The Politics of Curriculum and Testing.* New York: Falmer.

Smitherman, Geneva. (1977). *Talkin and Testifyin: The Language of Black America.* Boston: Houghton Mifflin.

———. (ed.) (1981). *Black English and the Education of Black Children and Youth.* Detroit: Wayne State University Press.

———. (1987). "Opinion: Toward the Development of a National Language Policy." *College English* 49: 302–317.

———. (1991). "What Is Africa to Me?: Language Ideology and African Americans." *American Speech* 66: 115–132.

————. (1994). *Black Talk: Words and Phrases for the Hood to the Amen Corner.* Boston: Houghton Mifflin.

Spears, Arthur. (1982). "The Black English Semi-Auxiliary Come." *Language* 58: 850–872.

Steele, C.; Spencer, S. J.; and Lynch, M. (1993). "Self-Image Resilience: The Role of Affirmational Resources." *Journal of Personality and Social Psychology* 64: 885–896.

Stewart, William A. (1967). "Sociolinguistic Factors in the History of American Negro Dialects." *Florida FL Reporter* 5: 11, 22, 24, 26.

Stockman, Ida. (1986). "Language Acquisition in Culturally Diverse Populations: The Black Child as a Case Study." In O. Taylor (ed.), *Nature of Communication Disorders in Culturally and Linguistically Diverse Populations,* pp. 117–155. San Diego, Calif.: College Hill Press.

————. (1996). "Phonological Development and Disorders in African American Children." In Alan Kamhi et al. (eds), *Communication Development and Disorders in African American Children: Research, Assessment, and Intervention,* pp. 117–153. Baltimore: Brookes.

Stockman, Ida, and Vaughn-Cooke, Faye. (1989). "Addressing New Questions about Black Children's Language." In R. Fasold and D. Schiffrin (eds.), *Language Change and Variation,* pp. 274–300. Amsterdam: John Benjamins.

Stratton, R. E. (1984). "Response No. 4 to Thomas J. Farrell." *College Composition and Communication* 35: 468–469.

Tannen, Deborah. (1982). "Oral and Literate Strategies in Spoken and Written Narratives." *Language* 58: 1–21.

Taylor, Orlando. (1971). "Response to Social Dialects and the Field of Speech." In *Sociolinguistics: A Cross Disciplinary Perspective,* pp. 13–20. Washington, D.C.: Center for Applied Linguistics.

Taylor, Orlando L., and Payne, Kay T. (1983). "Culturally Valid Testing: A Practical Approach." *Topics in Language Disorders* 3(3): 93–105.

Torrey, Jane. (1972). *The Language of Black Children in the Early Grades.* New London, Conn.: Department of Psychology, Connecticut College.

Trudgill, Peter. (1983). *On Dialect.* New York: New York University Press.

Tucker, G. Richard, and Lambert, Wallace E. (1972). "White and Negro Listeners' Reactions to Various American-English Dialects." In Joshua A. Fishman (ed.), *Advances in the Sociology of Language,* Vol. 2, pp. 175–184. The Hague: Mouton.

Turner, Lorenzo. (1949). *Africanisms in the Gullah Dialect.* Chicago: University of Chicago Press.

Tyack, D., and Cuban, L. (1995). *Tinkering toward Utopia.* Cambridge: Harvard University Press.

Valdés, G. (1996). *Con Respeto.* New York: Teachers College Press.

Vaughn-Cooke, F. V. (1987). "Are Black and White Vernaculars Diverging?" *American Speech* 62: 12–31.

Washington, Julie, and Craig, Holly. (1994). "Dialectal Forms during Discourse of Poor, Urban, African American Preschoolers." *Journal of Speech and Hearing Research,* 37(4): 816–823.

Weinreich, Uriel. (1953). *Languages in Contact.* The Hague: Mouton.

Weldon, Tracey. (1994). "Variability in Negation in African American Vernacular English." *Language Variation and Change* 6(3): 359–397.

Williams, Robert (ed.). (1975). *Ebonics: The True Language of Black Folks.* St. Louis: Robert Williams and Associates.

Wilson, W. J. (1981). *The Declining Significance of Race.* Chicago: University of Chicago Press.

———. (1987). *The Truly Disadvantaged.* Chicago: University of Chicago Press.

———. (1996). *When Work Disappears: The World of the New Urban Poor.* New York: Knopf

Winford, D. (1992). "Another Look at the Copula in Black English and Caribbean Creoles." *American Speech* 67, 21–60.

Wolfram, Walt. (1969). *A Sociolinguistic Description of Detroit Negro Speech.* Washington, D.C.: Center for Applied Linguistics.

———. "The Relationship of White Southern Speech to Vernacular Black English." *Language* 50: 498–527.

———. (1982). "Language Knowledge and Other Dialects." *American Speech* 57:3–18.

———. (1993). "Research to Practice: A Proactive Role for Speech-Language Pathologists in Sociolinguistic Education." *Language Speech and Hearing Services in Schools* 24: 181–85

Wolfram, Walt, and Fasold, Ralph. (1974). *Social Dialects in American English.* Englewood Cliffs, N.J.: Prentice-Hall.

Wolfson, Nessa. (1976). "Speech Events and Natural Speech." *Language in Society* 5: 81–96.

Wyatt, Toya. (1995). "Language Development in African American English Child Speech." *Linguistics and Education* 7: 7–22.

———. (1996). "Acquisition of the African American English Copula." In Alan Kamhi et al. (eds), *Communication Development and Disorders in African American Children: Research, Assessment, and Intervention,* pp. 95–113. Baltimore: Brookes.

Zentella, A. C. (1981). *Hablamos Los Dos—We Speak Both: Growing Up Bilingual in El Barrio.* Ph.D. diss., University of Pennsylvania.

INDEX